Way of the
WELL WOMAN

A GUIDE BOOK TO
FINDING PEACE AND TRUE LOVE

CATHERINE FENDIG

LINKPOINT PUBLISHING

Linkpoint Publishing

P.O. Box 20211

Saint Simons Island, Georgia 31522

(912) 399-4826

Visit our Web site at www.catherinefendig.com

ISBN 978-0-9667971-3-8

Library of Congress Control Number: 2012950686

Layout and design by Vancouver Desktop Publishing Centre.

Printed in the U.S.A.

WAY OF THE WELL WOMAN
is dedicated to
God and my husband Cap who have given me
the experience of finding true love.

ACKNOWLEDGEMENTS

I would like to thank the following people for their contributions to *WAY OF THE WELL WOMAN:*

To God, My Heavenly Father; to Jesus Christ, My Heavenly Husband and the Holy Spirit, without whom I would not be here and who have collaboratively and patiently loved, healed, and led me.

To Cap Fendig, my loving husband and friend, whose care, support, and wisdom have greatly contributed to my life. Thank you for being there at all times. You have given me the gift of true love in a marriage. I could not have done this without you.

To my children and grandchildren: Christina, Mary Ellyse, David, Kayla, Chandler, Carter, and Lu Lu, who have given me great joy and extra reasons to *"fight the good fight and run the race."* To all of my family and friends for continuing to teach me the meaning of love.

To Beth H. Evans, for her editing, for her experience and wisdom in living, and for her flare with words and details. To Patty Osborne for her excellent layout, print management and typesetting skills. To Debbie Martinez Brannam for her eagle eye and proofreading skills.

To my many teachers, near and far, in high places and low, who have shown me another way to think, live, and love. To the Reverend Wright Culpepper, for ministering God's Word with love and compassion and reaching out to many lost sheep. To Pastor David Yarborough and Pastor Jay Hanson, for being great examples of church leaders and for reaching out to numerous abused women who don't even attend church.

To Kathleen Pierce, for being a sister, friend, cheerleader, and inspiration. To David Brantley, for being an angel in disguise to many. To Marilou and Pat, for their friendship, love, and support, and for a writer's library.

Thank you to Jean, Carol, Jan, Gloria, Dee, BJ, Todd, Debbie, Helen, Julie, Valerie, Linda, Joyce, Gabby, Michele, Cathleen, Tully, Bernie and Cathy, Jeanette and Abe, Athena, Travis, Sandy, Meg, Robin, Reba, Kimberly, Teresa, Cindy, Christine, Chad, and my many recovery friends. I'd be lost without you. To my other friends in recovery who didn't make it, but through whose pain and relapses I am reminded of the truth and the need to stay sober. *You didn't die in vain.*

THE CHOICES

I choose to live by choice,
not by chance.

I choose to make changes,
not excuses.

I choose to be useful,
not used.

I choose to excel,
not compete.

I choose self-esteem,
not self-pity.

I choose to listen to the inner voice,
not the random opinion of others.

The choice is mine and I choose to surrender
to the will of God . . .

For in surrendering, I am victorious!!!
                                —*Unknown Author*

THE PARADOXES

From weakness (adversity) comes strength . . .

We forgive to be forgiven . . .

You've got to give it away to keep it . . .

We suffer to get well . . .

We surrender to win . . .

We die to live . . .

From dependence we found independence . . .

From darkness comes light . . .

This poem appeared in Abigail Van Buren column in response to a woman who had had a bad childhood and then married and stayed in an abusive relationship for twelve years. She said she stayed because she was programmed to believe the way she did about herself.

AFTER A WHILE

"After a while you learn the subtle difference between
holding a hand and chaining a soul,

And you learn that love doesn't mean leaning and
company doesn't mean security,

And you begin to learn that kisses aren't contracts and
presents aren't promises,

And you begin to accept your defeats with your head up
and your eyes open, with the grace of an adult, not the
grief of a child,

And you learn to build all your roads on today because
tomorrow's ground is too uncertain for plans.

After a while you learn that even sunshine burns if you get
too much.

So plant your own garden and decorate your own soul,
instead of waiting for someone to bring your flowers.

And you learn that you really can endure...

That you really are strong,
And you really do have worth."

—*Veronica Shoffstall*

CONTENTS

Appendices . . .

QUESTIONNAIRE

When we come out of neglectful and dysfunctional homes, we tend to unconsciously seek out mates who can recreate the abusive treatment that was familiar to us in childhood. Often, what we learn in childhood we carry on into relationships in adulthood. Until we heal, we usually hang on to the behaviors and attitudes we learned early in life.

Answer the following questions, which will help you decide if you have any of the common characteristics of an abused woman:

- Do I not want to be who I am?
- Do I run from my pain?
- Do I have love mixed up with sex and being desired by men?
- Do I get paralyzed with fear?
- Do I have difficulty speaking up for myself?
- Do I feel unsafe?
- Am I addicted to the adrenalin rush of chaos and crisis in my life?
- Do I act like a victim?
- Am I unable to stop repeating bad relationship patterns?
- Do I have low self-esteem?
- Do I do self-destructive things?
- Am I harsh, critical, and condemning of myself?

- Do I feel overly responsible for other peoples' problems.

- Do I feel everything is my fault? Do I apologize incessantly?

- Am I unable to set boundaries?

- Do I feel guilty standing up for myself?

- Do I isolate to deal with my loneliness?

- Is my morality confused? Have I slept with the wrong person on impulse or lust, and then married him to make it right?

- Do I do in adulthood what I learned in childhood, even though I swore I would make things different?

- Have I repeatedly involved myself with abusive, insensitive, and unavailable men despite my fear of abandonment and a dependent personality?

- Have my best attempts at change and healing left me powerless over my unmanageable life?

- Do I continuously find myself moving in the opposite direction of my dreams?

- Am I desperate because I do not know either God or love in my life?

If you answered yes to any of the above questions, read on. This study guide will help you explore ways to heal and change the characteristics and behaviors referred to above.

INTRODUCTION

Behavior is a mirror in which everyone
displays his image.

—Goethe

S ome of you are reading this book because you read *Becoming a
Well Woman*, which is the story of my journey from abusive relationships to finding true love. But I will provide a little background
here for those who have not read my first book and do not know
anything about me.

I grew up with a father who raged and a mother who drank. I
was not closely monitored, and was abused sexually by three different predators by the time I reached puberty. I experienced emotional and physical abuse at the hands of babysitters. I learned first-
hand about the instability and chaos that rules a home filled with
rage and alcohol. I learned to trust no one, to stay silent at all costs,
to stuff my feelings, to never stand up for myself, to take on more
responsibility than I could handle, to love conditionally, and to tell
white lies to cover up my home life.

Not surprisingly, I grew into an adult who lacked the skills
required for healthy relationships. In fairly short order, I went
through five marriages (and five divorces), with numerous abusive
relationships in between. Ignoring all the red flags, I repeatedly got
involved with abusive, emotionally unavailable men, always thinking it would be better the next time around, and always suffering
through dramatic breakups, abandonment, and devastating pain.
The men's names changed, but the result was always the same: I

was a serial marry-er who used drinking, drugging, and food to medicate my feelings.

They say insanity is doing the same thing over and over again and expecting different results, and that's exactly what I did.

I have learned that many of my past behaviors and characteristics are common to people who grew up in neglectful, dysfunctional homes. I suffered from feelings of low self-esteem, inadequacy, and unworthiness. I quickly judged and criticized myself. I thought that if I tried harder, I could be perfect. I always took responsibility for others; always tried to control outcomes of unpredictable events; and I was always angry or fearful when things didn't go the way I thought would be best or safest for me.

I isolated and felt uneasy around others. Often, I had trouble expressing honestly how I felt or what I thought. I was desperate to be liked, and was not honest about *yes* and *no* answers when people asked me to do things. As an approval-seeking people-pleaser, I often sacrificed who I was to become what I thought others wanted me to be. I was not able to share my true feelings if they contradicted someone else's for fear of angering them. I was intimidated by angry people. I often felt anxious and upset in the face of even mild criticism.

My life was a series of crises. I had no idea what it would be like to live a normal life. I lived as a victim, and was attracted to other victims in my love life and other relationships. I confused love with pity, and choose to love people I thought I could fix.

I denied, minimized, or repressed the traumas I had suffered as a child, unaware that doing that affected me negatively as an adult. Sometimes I reacted with overwhelming panic, anxiety, or fear and didn't know why. I was terrified of rejection and abandonment, and often I stayed in a job or a relationship that was harmful. I felt panicky when someone close to me was silent or emotionally absent.

I fantasized that danger could result from something coming down the pike, which made me hyper-vigilant, needing to be in control of everything going on, and overreacting to situations in which I had no control.

I was impulsive and unable to wait on God for His guidance, so I settled for less than what I really wanted by doing things without thought, making commitments I regretted later. My life was a never-ending experience of trying to clean up one mess after another.

As you can see, feeling plagued by fear, suicidal thoughts, self-abusive behaviors—such as drinking, using drugs, and smoking—feeling powerless, and being victimized over and over again, were just some of the results of the abuse and neglect in my childhood. The problem was, I had no clue why I kept doing things I did not want to do, and I didn't know how to change.

It is estimated that 21-million women—1/3 of the women in the United States—are in unhealthy and abusive relationships, and are experiencing emotional abuse. Abuse of any kind contributes to the death of one's spirit, and I was one of those women.

Finally, after narrowly escaping an abusive, violent relationship, and watching my life fall apart one more time, I reached a new level of pain and despair. Just when I thought I couldn't go on anymore, I met a woman named Ruth, who became my mentor in recovery. Ruth led me to Pastor Hart, who conducted a Bible study. Through his guidance and teaching, I found wisdom, and practical ways to apply that wisdom in my daily life. Between those Christian principles and the program of sobriety I followed, the healing work and subsequent miracles of understanding, growth, change, and transformation began.

As I followed the steps discussed in this book and healed, I gradually came to know who I was, and I became authentic and real. I've lost the desperate desire for inappropriate men or for any relationship at all. I have traveled a great distance in healing from alcohol, drugs, sex, relationships, and an eating disorder. I've had to learn to love myself, which includes learning to protect myself. God has given me a healthy life, one with meaning and purpose. He often uses my past to help others who are hurting from similar, painful beginnings in life. Through my spiritual journey, I discovered what had been preventing me from finding true love and how to fix that.

There is something very important that I need to tell you: To receive the benefits of healing and change, I had to set aside a sacred time during which I focused just on myself and God. I made a commitment to stay single for a season, to put God into the empty space inside instead of a relationship. That allowed me to remain focused on my growth and recovery, rather than to become distracted by someone else's needs, wants, hang-ups, past baggage, addictions, sexual infidelity, anger issues, and selfish desires—i.e., by another ill-fated relationship.

During that time of focusing just on myself and God, I grew spiritually without being sidetracked! And by honoring that season of God-focus, I learned some amazing things. What I had thought of as love was not love at all. It was codependency; it was abusive relationships heavily disguised as love.

My journey of healing and change led me into a wonderful, healthy relationship with a man. Cap and I have been married for over a decade at the time of publishing this book. I've had my share of hardships in recent years, between ailing parents and family members with alcohol and drug abuse problems, but I've had the blessing of a partner who stays present, available, and supportive. Cap is a godly man with integrity and character, with a deep love for God, his family, his community, and this country. He has been trustworthy and my best friend, loving me in ways only God could inspire.

I know from my personal experiences that there is a spiritual solution to the cycle of abusive relationships and to finding true, lasting love. This solution will work for you, too, for God is calling wounded women to come home to Him. We are being raised up as a new breed of spiritual warriors: *Well Women*.

So let's get started. Each chapter in this book focuses on a principle of recovery and a related piece of Scripture. Each contains suggestions for applying its principle to your own life. In each chapter, I share an experience from my own life about how that step healed me. There are also exercises, thoughts, and questions to help you discover some of your own truths and see how each of these principles can be applied to your own healing journey. At the conclusion of each chapter, there is a relevant prayer.

This guide book is about learning to love. All you will need for this course is a pen and a commitment to focus on yourself and God, for now. Some may enjoy having a user-friendly Bible on hand for checking out the Scripture references. And some may ask a friend, someone with whom you can share confidentially and openly, to accompany you on this journey. Maybe you know another woman who is seeking her own healing from abuse and addictions, and maybe you will invite her to be your study guide partner. Or maybe you will choose to share this journey with a clergyperson, a therapist, or just a trusted friend. It is fine to use this study guide on your own. But I know that another person's encouragement and prayer support can help us in our blind spots and "keep us honest" through accountability. And, of course, walking this walk with another recovering woman can provide marvelous opportunities to support each other back to wholeness.

As you practice these principles, be prepared to experience an unseen God putting people and situations into your life when you need them most for healing, love, support, and breakthroughs! God intimately knows the desires, thoughts, and intentions of your heart. Whatever you are facing, He knows how to reach you and awaken you. Each of us has a divine destiny that God has specifically created for us, and He is waiting for you to claim yours. You can be an over-comer and a victor. You can become a *Well Woman*.

I invite you to open the door to the new and transforming destiny God created you to walk in. He's calling out to you! He can and will, if you seek Him. I'll be standing by in prayer for you as you continue on your healing journey.

With love,
Catherine Fendig

Making Peace with God . . .

Understanding is the reward of faith.
Therefore, seek not to understand that
thou mayest believe, but believe that thou
mayest understand.

—*Aurelius Augustinus*

The first three steps toward recovery are
interdependent and form a solid foundation, like
the three legs holding up a stool. First, we identify
the **problem**: powerlessness. Next, we look at the
solution: God's power. And then we make the
decision: to explore and apply the solution.

ONE

Powerlessness

Admit It: Confess your need for help, that you and your life are unmanageable. Write a brief description of how you got to where you are, beginning with your first relationship with your dad and/or mom. (*Romans 7:18*)

Sir Winston Churchill once said, "Men stumble over the truth from time to time, but most pick themselves up and hurry off as if nothing happened."

Looking at the truth about our lives can feel overwhelming. In order to change where we are, we have to become *aware* of where we are and then deal with it. When we recognize our brokenness and powerlessness, we become changeable and teachable. Admissions like, "I can't handle this!" "I give up!" "I need help!" all signal the beginning of growth. Looking at ourselves honestly is not a call to judge or condemn ourselves. It is only an invitation to look at where we are and admit that we are powerless to change on our own. In this step, we start identifying the causes of the behaviors we can't control.

We need to have courage and not "... hurry off as if nothing has happened" because the way *out* of our pain is *through* it. Finally recognizing our powerlessness to change someone else, we turn our attention to where we *can* effect change, and that is in ourselves.

We must do our best to eliminate distractions in early recovery.

We need to avoid the lure of those things that would encourage us to "hurry off as if nothing has happened." I invite you to consider setting aside a season of your life as your prep time. Commit to no dating or intimate relationships for a time such as one year, and use that as sacred time to develop *yourself* and let God prepare you for what is to come. Prep time is that time when you would be mending the fishnet, if you were a disciple—strengthening it, cutting out the weak spots—as we read in Luke 5:1-6. Put your love life in God's hands to be developed at a later date. When you do so, you position yourself to receive God's best in God's own timing. Focus on your own growth and recovery.

In the same way that alcoholics use alcohol to numb themselves and avoid dealing with life, love addicts use unhealthy relationships. The substance we use (our drug) is another person; it can also be an abusive relationship, which we have called love.

Before I got into recovery, I moved around the country a lot. Moving from place to place was my way of coping with the wreckage of my life and the bad choices I made. Every time I experienced a broken relationship and the abandonment and betrayal that followed, I sought to escape the pain. Feeling ashamed of my life, I began trying to hide my past. I kept secrets. Sometimes, I moved to another state, hoping for a fresh start, with the unrealistic thought that, by changing locations, I could become someone different.

Each time I met new people or began a new relationship, I feared that people would discover how defective I was. What would they think if they found out I had been divorced multiple times, that I had been repeatedly abused by men, and that I was an alcoholic? What if someone found out I had been molested frequently as a child? False pride kept me in darkness, ignorance, and fear, and I often lied about my past.

After my last sick relationship, in which I was physically assaulted and could have been killed, I reached a level of pain that finally broke through my thick wall of denial. I finally realized that the walls I'd built to keep people from seeing *in* had also prevented me from seeing *out*. When I first began working with my mentor and I was asked to write about the reality of where I was in my life, I was terrified of disclosing my truth. I was overwhelmed with shame. My mentor had me do a relationship inventory, a written history of the experiences I had had with men, starting with my father and up to the present. If I was going to take this first step toward recovery, I had to admit to the abuse, all the failed marriages, and the sexual assaults—all of which had left me feeling unworthy of a good life.

Once I completed writing my relationship inventory, I shared its contents with my mentor. As I began doing so, I had to remember to breathe in. My hands felt shaky. Yet, when I finished saying out loud what I had hidden for years, I noticed that she wasn't the least bit fazed by what I had shared. I asked her, "Does this shock you?" and she calmly said, "Now I understand. You did the best you could with what you had and what you knew. It's going to be all right."

She didn't judge me and or act like I was the first or the last woman to admit to such things. She helped me see the connection between what I had been taught by my caregivers and abusers in childhood, and the men I chose in adulthood. I felt great relief and love wash over my spirit as the walls of false pride and shame broke down into transparency. The beginnings of self-acceptance began in that honest exchange with my mentor. That night, I learned that, as Dr. Phil says, "You can't fix what you won't acknowledge."

Ask yourself this: If you were to choose one person to spend the rest of your life with, would you choose yourself?

Abandonment

Most of us have strong abandonment issues. In an unhealthy relationship, we can be physically abandoned by a partner who leaves us; or psychologically abandoned by emotionally unavailable men. When that happens to us, we become so fixated on what the other person is doing and on our pain that we lose sight of the ways in which we have abandoned ourselves in the process

Feelings of abandonment can develop early in childhood when

we never know, one day to the next, if our parents are going to be there for us, either physically or emotionally. Having felt unimportant as children, we tend to grow up and choose partners who will also treat us as if we are unimportant. Avoiding the experience of being abandoned again becomes more important, in our adult relationships, than dealing with issues or conflict. Hoping to avoid further abandonment, we try to be perfect, and we put all the focus on our partner. Our insecurities, and the fear of being rejected or alone, can set us up to stay in detrimental situations.

Let's go back to the roots of our abandonment. In the space below, list the times you felt abandoned by your parents or caregivers. List any details you can remember, such as how old you were at the time of your memory, and the place where the abandonment occurred. Write what you felt and thought at the time:

_____

_____

_____

_____

_____

_____

_____

_____

_____

Now answer the following questions:

- Is any relationship worth being used and abused in over and over?

- How many more heartaches, heartbreaks, disappointments, and disillusionments do you want to have?

- What are you really looking for in life? Is it love, security, and companionship?

- Is the pain of staying in a bad relationship less than the pain of being alone and facing your pain from the past?

Man was never meant to fix and fill the hole around the wounded child inside of us. That space can only be filled by God, our Heavenly Father. Most of us get stuck and turn away from God because we project onto Him the neglect we experienced from our earthly fathers. Until we make the distinction between the two, we live as abandoned orphans. A loving, caring father provides, protects, and loves with kindness, comfort, and guidance.

God is the loving Father we all seek. You can turn to God and rely on His promise that He will never abandon you! Others may mistreat you or leave you, but God never will. He loves you and wants you to be part of His family forever. God tells us that nothing can separate us from His love. In Romans 8:38-39, He promises that neither death, life, angels, principalities, powers, things present, things to come, height, nor depths can keep us from His love.

When someone you love betrays your trust and turns his back on you, take comfort in Jesus's promise in John 14:18: He will come to you and will not abandon you as orphans. If you are heartbroken, devastated, or depressed because a man left you, mistreated you, cheated on you, abused you, and/or wouldn't meet your needs, consider looking at these heartaches and disappointments as a means of getting closer to what you really wish for. You could decide that "Rejection is God's protection!" Wouldn't you feel better thinking that the relationship ended because God was protecting and saving you for something better and more appropriate, even though you didn't know He was there for you?

You can decide that what seems to be another setback is really a stepping stone to what you truly want in life. *Rejection is God's protection. God has a better plan for your future!* Dale Carnegie once said, ". . . happiness doesn't depend upon who you are or what you have; it depends upon what you think."

Real Love

Real love brings security into our life. Believing that true love and lasting security exist, and that they can be ours, is hard if we don't know what love really is.

Pain comes from desperately looking for love in all the wrong places. Peace comes from finding real love. God teaches us what real love is through His Word and through our experiences with Him. Once we have found Him, we can recognize His love, receive it, and learn to express it in our lives. But until we realize what God's love is like, we are closed off from receiving it. The key is to take the time to learn *what love is* and *what love isn't*, according to God. As we open the doors of our hearts to Him, our past disappointments fade and our trust in His goodness grows.

To learn about real love, compare what you think it is to what God says it is in 1 Corinthians 13:4-13; 1 Peter 4:8; and I John 4:18. Then read 1 Corinthians 13:4-10, which sums up the things love does *not* do. The following are things love *does* according to God's Word:

> Love . . . suffers long.
> Love . . . rejoices in truth.
> Love . . . bears all things.
> Love . . . believes all things.
> Love . . . hopes all things.
> Love . . . endures all things.
> Love . . . abides now.
> Love . . . covers a multitude of sins.
> Perfect Love . . . casts out fear.

The following are things love does not do, according to God's Word:

> Love is not . . . envious.
> Love is not . . . puffed up.
> Love is not . . . easily provoked.
> Love does not . . . vaunt itself.
> Love does not . . . behave unseemly.
> Love does not . . . seek its own.
> Love does not . . . rejoice in iniquity.
> Love thinks no . . . evil.
> Love never . . . fails.
> Love works no . . . ill to his neighbour.

Love is a verb; it is an action that is based on making a choice. Love means thinking the best of a person and wishing for others success even greater than your own. Love does not lead to anger; it takes anger away. Love doesn't yell back. It is consistent, predictable, and secure. It can mean humbling yourself, not putting yourself above others. Love doesn't get disappointed in the other person. Love can mean behaving in ways that are *right*, if not necessarily comfortable or reflective of what you want. Love is about doing for others and not making it all about yourself. Love means being truthful and open, even when doing so embarrasses us. Love offers untold second chances. Love hopes, and knows the future will be good, even if things looks bad right now; and love means that you stand for the other person, regardless of his failures or successes.

By now, I hope you are reflecting on some of your past experiences and what you thought love was. Maybe you chose some of your relationships still not knowing what love is, what it looks like, and how it acts. We can use God's description of love as a standard by which to gauge real love and as a means of measuring how lovingly we are behaving, as well. It is essential for us to learn to recognize the real expressions of love so that we are no longer deceived into accepting abuse while labeling that love.

Relationship Inventory

Taking a relationship history helps us compare God's description of love to what we have actually experienced in our relationships. Seeing discrepancies between these two experiences helps us discover what brought us to the problems we face today. In Chapter One, we acknowledge what the problem is in order to get to work on it.

Briefly write down your key relationships with men throughout your life, beginning with your father until now. Look at each man, the role he played and what he meant to you. Write down the most significant things that happened in the relationship, and how you felt about it. This will help you begin to see your patterns in relationships more clearly.

Person	His Role in my Life	What Happened	How it Ended

By actually writing down the facts of what happened in our relationships, we often see that we had not really allowed ourselves to view them accurately. If we were in denial, we were clinging to how we *wished* things were, rather than looking at how they actually were.

Why are so many of us blind to reality? The answer may be rooted in childhood. When a child's situation feels out of control and too frightening to cope with, she often survives by fantasizing about what she *wishes* were true rather than focusing on what is actually going on. That is a form of denial, and, in childhood, it can help us survive. But as adults, practicing denial robs us of our ability to see and deal with reality and, therefore, to make healthy changes in our lives.

To stop living in fantasy and to look at what is actually occurring in our lives, we do a Fantasy/Reality Checklist. Make up two separate lists, one containing the *What I Want to Have Happen in My Life,* the other listing *What is Actually Happening in My Life.* You can create a Fantasy/Reality assessment for any aspect of your life that is not working for you. Use this assessment as a way to identify major areas of denial. Fill out the following list:

Fantasy	Reality
What I want to have happen:	What IS actually happening:
1.	1.
2.	2.
3.	3.
4.	4.

By looking at the lists, you can readily see where you're in denial and not living in real time. When we look at what is *actually* happening, instead of at some imagined present or potential future, we can make new choices that will be effective. By focusing our time and attention on building a real and solid present, we give our fantasies a chance to become future realities. The future is a string of moments unfolding out of the present. The future can't change the present; the present is what creates the future. By reviewing what you have written, you can make new choices from a place of empowerment.

Below is an example of a Fantasy/Reality Checklist, written by a woman in an abusive relationship:

Fantasy	Reality
What I want to have happen:	What IS actually happening:
1. Be treated with love and care	1. Beat up on me
2. To have him be sensitive to my needs	2. He is not there for me
3. To be heard and understood	3. He doesn't listen to me
4. To be protected	4. He hurts me
5. For him to be trustworthy	5. He is dishonest and deceitful
6. To have him do what he say	6. He says one thing and does another

This Fantasy/Reality Check List describes a person's love interest as neglectful, emotionally unavailable, and insensitive to the needs she identifies in Column One. Often, we stay in these broken relationships because we fantasize about what things could be like in the future "If he would change" (Column Two).

We may want a happy, peaceful home with a loving, committed, even-tempered partner; but if the person we're in a relationship with isn't capable of providing those things, then hanging onto the fantasy that, in the future, he may *become someone he isn't* will not get us what we need. Our fantasies can keep us from seeing what is actually happening in the present. The key is to: *Focus on the present and assess what is happening now, and then respond appropriately to reality.* It isn't possible to respond appropriately to a fantasy future that does not exist. Look over your reality check list and answer the following questions:

- Do you ignore your own needs?

- Are you responding to yourself, or do you run from yourself?

- How are you treating yourself in this situation?

- Does your partner's treatment of you reflect the way you treat yourself? (For example: Do *you* beat up on yourself? or Do *you* distance yourself from your feelings by eating, drinking, drugging, or any other self-destructive habits?)

- Are you able to see your part in choosing to get involved with/ stay in this situation?

- Are you volunteering to be the victim by staying in a relationship that doesn't meet your needs?

- Are you continuing to blame others for the unhappiness in your life?

Seeing what we do to perpetuate our patterns can give us a great sense of freedom. It can help us identify precisely what we need to do for ourselves. Instead of asking, *Why did* _____ *(the person) act this way toward me?* I can ask, *What can I learn from what happened?* By focusing on changing ourselves instead of someone else, our lives can progress, and we don't have to stay stuck in what has already happened.

A good recovery slogan is: "You spot it, you've got it!" Basically, this means that it is much easier to spot the negative in someone else than to see it in ourselves. Very often, what we resent in someone else's treatment of us is something we unconsciously do to ourselves, as well. When we choose to react to what someone else has done to us, we miss the real message.

But why would we treat ourselves badly? The answer can be found in the messages we heard repeatedly from our childhood caregivers about life and who we were. Over time, these bits of information became the "facts" by which we assessed ourselves and the world. But these "facts" were rooted not in truth, but in other peoples' warped ideas and perspectives. We adopted them without even thinking about them. For many of us, these ideas had negative impacts on our life and robbed us of self-esteem. Because of them, we may have made poor judgments or become drawn to others who would treat us badly, reflecting back to us the unworthiness we felt and believed about ourselves.

It's important that, as adults, we go back and identify some of the key messages we, as children, received and accepted as facts before we were old enough to discern if there was any truth in them. Examples of messages many of us heard thousands of times in childhood were:

"I am so ashamed of you."

"I am so disappointed in you."

"You're stupid."

"You don't know what you are talking about."

"You won't ever amount to anything."

"After all I've done for you, you're so ungrateful and selfish."

In the space below list some of the messages your caregivers gave you as a child:

1. _____

2. _____

3. _____

4. _____

To complete your Chapter One work of looking at the powerlessness, unmanageability, and denial in your life and relationships, answer the following questions as honestly as you can:

Powerlessness

- Are you willing to admit you are powerless over the way you were raised and the fact that your life became unmanageable as a consequence of abuse and neglect?

- List three effects of growing up in an alcoholic, addicted, or dysfunctional home. (Hint: any of the abused-woman traits found in the Appendices in the back of this book).

- How many of the common abused-woman traits or problems do you identify with in the list?

- What kind of self-destructive things are you doing now?

- In what ways do you run from or try to avoid pain?

- Do you speak to yourself harshly? Do you criticize and condemn yourself?

- Do you use food, sex, drugs, alcohol, work, gambling, or any other addictive behavior to an extreme? Are you powerless over these activities? (Give an example of how you are powerless.)

- What are the effects of your self-destructive habits?

- Have you been driven by a compulsion or obsession for another person that overpowered you and caused you to deny your own needs or fail to take care of yourself? (If so, detail how you denied your own needs.)

Unmanageability

- Are you taking responsibility for other peoples' problems? Describe:

- Have you let others take advantage of you?

- In what ways does your life feel out of control and unmanageable?

- What kind of chaos and crises have you had in your life?

- What is your definition of being unmanageable or having an unmanageable life? *(Ex - Letting your personal will run wild, never having any peace or rest, not trusting God and His results, and trying to control the uncontrollable.)*

- Do you still try to control people, places, and things by acting right, perfect, or manipulating others?

- Do you think you have power over other people and that you can control their actions and thoughts? Give an example:

- Are you letting the thoughts, feelings, and actions of others have power over yourself? Give an example:

- Do you wear yourself out worrying about pleasing others, wondering what they're thinking and if they're happy?

- Have your relationships created chaos, abuse, or turmoil in your life? Give an example:

- Have you hit your bottom in abusive relationships?

Denial

- In childhood, were you forced to depend on an abusive or neglectful parent for food and shelter?

- To survive as a child, did you ignore your feelings of shame, fear, and neglect?

- Did you monitor your parents' feelings or moods to determine how you should feel? Were you only happy when your parents were happy, and sad when they were sad? Give an example:

- How has being involved with abusive, insensitive, and unavailable men affected your life?

- Do you feel like a victim?

- Are you repeating bad relationship patterns?

- Do you lie to yourself and others?

- Have you put yourself in dangerous situations? Describe:

As we come out of denial and look at the reality of our lives, we can feel overwhelmed with shame, guilt, or embarrassment. We may wonder how to handle our shame for some of the things you've done. Shame is a useless emotion. Guilt is like a smoke alarm in our soul, signaling that we really do need to pay attention to some action/ behavior of ours and make changes. But shame produces nothing life-changing or life-enhancing; it has no use or value in life. Looking at the truth will be painful, but it is the beginning of a recovery that can change your life and lead to freedom from the past. You are not alone. God is here with you and will bring others who are also on this journey into your life, as well. The good news is, the more of a mess your life has been, the more you can be used by God to help others once He cleans you up. Don't be afraid to admit the truth in Chapter One: *The greater your mess, the greater your miracle!*

Scriptures Related To Chapter One:

Romans 7:18	Deuteronomy 31:8	2 Corinthians 12:9-10
Isaiah 41:10	Zephaniah 3:17	2 Corinthians 6:14

Prayer for Chapter One:

Dear God,
> *Please help me! Amen.*

TWO

Belief

Believe It: Acknowledge (recognize) that God is greater than you and that He wants you to live. (*Philippians 2:13*)

Hope arrives and gives birth to faith as we open our minds and become willing to believe that a Power bigger than ourselves can enable us to grow in love, health, and grace. God wants you to live in victory and to see that help is available. All we need to do is accept what God has to offer. The way and the means will be shown and given, one step at a time.

Our second step in recovery asks us to recognize that there is this God/Power greater than ourselves in the universe. In this chapter, we become willing to accept that help is available and to trust that God wants to heal us. In the last chapter, our first step, we admitted our powerlessness, hopelessness, and feelings of being beaten down. Now, we accept the idea that God is a Power greater than ourselves and we begin to build the spiritual foundation for our growth, change, and healing. By taking this risk and choosing to trust God, we become open to the possibility of the miraculous healing of our old patterns of behavior that we could not change on our own power. With God, we see that we can gradually become the person we were meant to be.

When my last abusive relationship ended, I felt devastated by my hopeless situation. After my partner's violent attempts to hurt me, I knew I had to get out of the situation. I asked for help in packing up my household possessions while he was at work. Then I moved my things into my storage unit, and within twenty-four hours, I was homeless and feeling hopeless about how to move forward. I had no idea what my future would hold, and I was frightened.

In fact, I was overwhelmed by the situation. I was disoriented. I had lost my home, relationship, and footing overnight. I didn't have enough money to get another place immediately. Unanswered questions raced around and around in my head: Could I get back on my feet again? How would I provide for myself and my daughter? What if my ex came after me? Would I be safe? How would I get my mail? With no home phone, no cell phone, and no address, how would I stay in touch with people? Where was I going to sleep? Could I do my job under the stress of this situation?

Looking at just my own limited resources and my broken, wearied self, I feared what would happen to me and wondered if I could make it. Our second step in recovery, belief, provided the key to walking through the mess I was in. Applying belief, I chose to recognize that there is a God and that He is greater than I am. I also, through faith, believed that He wanted me to live.

I realized that fear and anxiety were diminishing my ability to hear God's direction. When I accepted and chose to apply the principle of chapter two to my predicament, the first result was peace. Peace came over me and replaced fear.

It was necessary to *choose* to believe that God had a way out of my situation and to *choose* to believe that, if I followed His lead, He would put me back on solid ground. I certainly had a better chance of perceiving God's direction through a peaceful spirit and demeanor than from a position of panic. I *decided to believe*—that God could and would help me.

Immediately after making that choice to believe, I felt calmer and steadier. Nothing had changed except my point of view, yet now I had hope. The next day at work, I took my lunch with a coworker who was becoming a friend. No one at work knew anything about my personal life and the events that had just transpired. But, for some reason, I confided in her about them. She insisted that I stay at her home for the next two weeks while I figured out what to do. She wouldn't let me pay for anything, suggesting that I save my paychecks to get an apartment. She let me use her home phone number and forward my mail to her address.

She and I spent evenings after work cooking healthy dinners, and she comforted me in ways I desperately needed. All of this unfolded from the moment I chose to believe God could help me, and would if I looked to Him.

Most of us have made men the God of our lives. We have put a man in God's place as the first one we look to for love, protection, provision, and guidance. But a man cannot take the place of God, and obsessively wanting to be wanted by an unavailable or abusive man creates an out-of-control, unmanageable life. People in recovery programs often say, "What you place before God, you will lose." It is important to ask ourselves, "Who have we made God in our life?" Was it a boyfriend, husband, friends, children?

God requires us to put *Him* first. When we sacrifice the reality of who we are in order to appease someone else or to avoid confronting the truth of our situation, we lose ourselves in the process. Often in an attempt to avoid being abandoned, we stop being honest and being ourselves. Eventually, what we fear comes upon us, and we are left alone, having forsaken ourselves and God. We are to learn to be true to ourselves and to God first.

In the story of Abraham and Isaac (Genesis 22:1-9), God tested Abraham's faith and obedience to God's will. Abraham proved his obedience and faithfulness to God by not questioning God's request that he offer up his son as a sacrifice to God. God did not intend to actually kill Abraham's son; He only wanted to know the depth of Abraham's devotion. Abraham passed this test through his unquestioning willingness to put God first in his life.

Now ask yourself, "Is God first above all else in my life?"

Remember our earlier definition of insanity? *Repeating the same behavior, always expecting different results.* It is in that sense, that repeatedly linking up with the same type of unavailable, abusive men is insanity: *This time around, this unavailable, abusive man will be just the right one. This time, I will manage to change or fix him and make the relationship work.*

Our second step of recovery, Belief, tells us that there is a solution to always being drawn to the wrong man and doing things we don't want to do. That solution lies in doing things a new way—God's way. And all we need to say is, "Okay, I'll try it. I'll look to God as a loving, not condemning, God, who will teach me to live in a healthy way."

Our problem isn't a lack of willpower and self-control. Our problem is that we have looked to everyone and everything BUT God, and God is our only solution. We have a problem in our minds and hearts the only solution to which is developing a relationship with God and following His lead into healing. When we learn to receive God's love and put Him first, we change how we act and what we choose to allow in our life. God can do in and through us what we could never do on our own.

For some of us, accepting that God exists and is the answer to our problem may be a challenge. You may be aware of how He has worked wonders in the lives of others, yet can't believe He'll do this for you. You may ask, "How can just believing actually change the seemingly impossible things of my life?" I can only tell you that this is a *faith* walk not a *logic* walk. Faith means believing without proof up front.

Some of us have trouble believing God because we have had such great difficulties in our lives. We ask, "Why did such unfair things happen in my childhood/adulthood?" It's easy to look at our difficulties and wonder if God is interested in us at all. How God can care about us but still let these things happen to us?

There are many things we won't understand while we are still here on earth. John 16:33 tells us, *"You will have tribulation, but be of good cheer; I have overcome the world."* God warns us to expect problems and troubles in our life. His Son certainly did! But God specifically says that, despite our tribulations, we can be of good cheer because He has overcome all of it.

In Deuteronomy 31:8, God says, *"I will not ever leave you or forsake you."* This means that God will be with us through whatever we have or will ever experience in life; He never leaves our side. We can rest in the knowledge that, in the end, there will be victory over our challenges. God's goodness and faithfulness will bring about His promise of sanity and restoration in our life.

Some of us think our unworthiness makes us undeserving of God's love and grace. Through Scripture, God explains that sin is "missing the mark." In God's eyes, we all "miss the mark" equally because God does not consider one sin to be bigger or smaller than any other. (James 2:10) We are all on a level playing field. The truth is, none of us deserves the goodness of what God gives us. No one can pray often enough or fast enough, or be committed enough to the Ten Commandments, or confess our faith well enough or often enough to EARN God's love.

God's love and grace are free gifts. They are given to all who turn to Him and believe in Him. They are not dependent on our performance. God's love and grace are simply ours for the asking. So whatever we did before now, no matter how unacceptable our lives are in our own eyes, we are qualified to receive God's love, acceptance, and grace. Period.

Recovery is a "God's-way walk," not a "self-will walk." As we seek to live more God-like lives, we naturally grow in faith and belief. As we experience God's miracles, gifts, and divine appointments, we come to know personally the reality of God's omnipotent goodness.

We need to learn how to seek God. In this second chapter, we are invited to believe in God as the loving Creator, the Higher Power who has the strength and authority to heal our lives—not through a religious experience, doctrine, or specific denomination, but through *a relationship with Him.* As an old proverb explains, "If you give a man a fish, he has one meal. If you teach them how to fish, he can feed himself for the rest of his life." Finding our individual relationship with God is like being taught to fish: God is the source of all wisdom, and, therefore, all we will ever need for the rest of our lives. God is available and accessible to us. He wants to reveal Himself to us.

The way to learn about God's truth, wisdom, and answers for our lives, is to read the manual He wrote for us, the Bible. It was given to us by our Creator and is filled with His basic instructions for us before leaving the earth. 2 Timothy 3:16-17 (NIV) says, *"All Scripture is God-breathed and is useful for teaching, rebuking, correcting and training in righteousness, so that the servant of God may be thoroughly equipped for every good work."* And 2 Peter 1:20-21 tells us that God uses men to write His Words for Him.

The Bible

The Bible is a spiritually powerful mystical book. I do not want to focus too much here on "just the facts, ma'am" about what the Bible contains. At the same time, I want to share with you some sense of the scope and range of the countless ways God reveals Himself to us through it. Just opening the Bible, you can experience God's presence and you can draw Him into your life. He will open your eyes and reveal the truth of what is written in the scriptures.

God's Word is our spiritual food. (Deuteronomy 8:3)
God's Word is right. (Psalm 33:4)
God's Word is true. (Psalm 119:160)
God's Word is pure. (Proverbs 30:5)
God's Word made the Heavens. (Psalm 33:6)
God's Word is listened to and obeyed by the Angels.
   (Psalm 103:20)
God's Word is sent to heal. (Psalm 107:20)
God's Word will cleanse your way. (Psalm 119:9)
God's Word is settled forever in Heaven. (Psalm 119:89)
God's Word is a light on our path. (Psalm 119:105)
God's Word accomplishes and doesn't return empty.
   (Isaiah 55:11)
God's Word breaks through all obstacles. (Jeremiah 23:29)
God's Word comes to pass. (Ezekiel 12:25)

God's Word is expressed through Christ. (John 1:14)

God's Word can't be silenced by any obstacles or resistance.
    2 Timothy 2:9)

God's Word is the sword of the spirit. (Ephesians 6:17)

God's Word is powerful and speaks deeply to the spirit.
    (Hebrews 4:12)

God's Word lives forever. (1 Peter 1:23)

Even though the Bible was written thousands of years ago, its truths and principles are timeless, giving answers to every question and need in our lives. It accurately describes both our potential and what causes our problems. Whatever our emotional state—whether we are sad, fearful, angry, overwhelmed, confused, alone—there is comfort and direction waiting to be found in its pages. It contains the greatest wisdom ever written regarding how humans really work, about relationships, marriage, family, health, healing, career, and even finances. Absolutely nothing is missing from it, and it will change your life forever.

The Bible is also a recorded history, an unfolding story of how God redeems and restores us through His saving grace and its leading character, Jesus. Originally, it was copied by hand very accurately by experienced scribes. Common knowledge has it that, of the thousands of copies made by hand before 1500, more than 5,300 Greek manuscripts from the New Testament alone still exist and resemble very closely the versions we have today. There are also more than 100 archeological finds and other historical records that confirm the accuracy of many of the Bible's descriptions of cities, battles, and rulers.

In 1455, the Bible became the first book ever to be printed on the Johannes Gutenberg's invention, the printing press with movable type. It is one of the first books ever translated out of its original language, and, today, the Bible has the largest circulation of any book in history. Billions of copies have been sold, with over 2,200 translations worldwide in over fifty countries. The Bible has survived against all odds and endless persecutions. Even though it was written over a 1,500-year time span, by different authors writing on three different continents, in three different languages, in differing literary styles, and on hundreds of controversial subjects, it has nevertheless maintained an amazing continuity of content. Only God could have done that! The statistics of no other book compares to this one.

The Bible is laid out in two major sections, the Old Testament and the New Testament. The Old Testament takes place up until 400 years before Christ. The New Testament starts with Christ's birth.

The Scriptures cover an amazing range of topics, from delivery and sacrifice to blessings and curses; from rebellions, to forgiveness and restoration. The stories cover a wide a range of topics, from family problems to adultery, obedience, loyalty, and faithfulness. You will find stories of repentance, of suffering, and God's faithfulness. And you will learn about communicating with God and worshiping Him. Above all, you will find in its pages God's wisdom, guidance, truth, joy, and His unspeakable love for us. As you find your own relationship with God through its pages, you will also find the courage and strength needed to love one another and to be faithful in the midst of suffering.

Why read the Bible? Roman 10:17 tells us: *So then faith comes by hearing, and hearing by the Word of God.* We want to read the Bible because we would not turn to a God we know nothing about, and in whom we have found no basis for trust. So we need to get a look at who God is, and it is in the Bible that we read of His qualities. There, God is described as faithful, truthful, enduring; kind, healing, protective; forgiving, invisible, omnipresent, powerful; our preserver and savior; as sovereign, wise, understanding; a comforter and companion who is impartial, gentle, merciful, dependable, and stable. Listed below are various names and descriptions of God and His nature found in the Bible:

God is MY CREATOR: God knows all and creates all and He is everywhere at all times. (Genesis 1:1-3)

God is I AM: He is the One who is. God never changes and His promises never fail. (Exodus 3:14)

God is MY SUPPLIER: God is all powerful. (Philippians 4:19)

God is OUR TOTAL AUTHORITY: God is sovereign over all. (1 Samuel 2:6-8)

God is MY PROVIDER: God meets all our needs. (Matthew 6:30)

God is MY HEALER: God can heal us. (Psalm 147:3, Psalm 103:3)

God is MY BANNER: God gives us victory. (Deuteronomy 20:3-4)

God is MY SANCTIFIER: God sets us apart as His own, cleanses us from our sins and helps us mature. (1 Peter 1:15-16)

God is MY RIGHTEOUSNESS: God imparts His righteousness to us. (Ezekiel 36:26-27, 2 Corinthians 5:21)

God is MY PEACE: God defeats our enemies to bring us peace. (John 14:27)

God is MY SHEPHERD: God protects, directs, leads and cares for His people. (Psalm 23:1-3)

God is MY COMPANION: God's abiding presence is accessible to all who love and obey Him. (Matthew 28:20)

As we learn and experience God's love for us, we personally begin to understand and experience the truth disclosed in 1 John 4:19: *"We love Him because He first loved us."*

Faith

True faith is the result of a living relationship with a loving God, who empowers us to do all that He asks of us. (2 Corinthians 3:4-5) God wants us to choose faith instead of doubt so that we will be blessed. (Romans 14:22-23) Moving in faith requires resting in the assurance that, regardless of what comes, God will make it right. Breaking through from fear to faith requires learning to trust God, learning about His character and His Word, and learning to wait for Him to work things out. Doing things according to God's will usually requires a faith walk.

During the course of our lives, there will be countless moments and challenges in which we will have to choose between faith or fear. If we are not growing in faith and the peace of God, we will be increasingly fearful. But Philippians 4:19 tells us that everything we need today shall be supplied to us. When we choose to trust God, we tap into a source greater than our own. God has everything at His disposal. He is our source of infinite, short-term and long-term supply. Our task is to align ourselves with God's will and to release fear and limited, negative thinking so that our lives can unfold and become all we were meant to be through God's lead and timing.

When circumstances are contrary to what we pray or ask for, we are being given the opportunity to practice faith and patience. God matures and develops our faith during the times when, despite our belief, we think our needs are not being met. God often sees that our even greater need is to wait on Him, to develop our faith, so that we will be ready and able to receive the promise when He knows the time is right. Faith requires believing *before* receiving. That's why it's called faith! Believe it first—because God said so—and, in His time and His way, it will materialize through your obedience.

God has dealt to each one of us a measure of faith. (Romans 12:3) The moment we turn to God, He gives us a starter portion of faith. Then, as we use what we have been given, God can give us even more. Faith grows through practice and patience and through the experience of seeing God at work in our own and others' lives.

You may well ask, "How can we believe what we can't see or know?" As mentioned earlier, faith comes by hearing. (Romans 10:7) In the Bible, we find story after story about how God came through in the lives of people who faced impossible challenges. Seeing God at work, in those stories, we find something to anchor our faith in.

Faith isn't just a message. Faith is *the behavior of believing* what God said and acting on that belief. Your inner spirit recognizes the truth found in God's Word and connects with it. That connection stimulates the measure of faith inside of you. The Word of God is alive. (John 1:1) When you connect your measure of faith with God's Word, the mystical and extraordinary can happen, just as we are promised in Hebrews 4:11: *God's Word is living and active and sharper than a two-edged sword.* It can penetrate and cut through all the doubt, pain, and confusion of our lives.

Scripture tells us that if we have faith even the size of a mustard seed (the very smallest of seeds), we can say, "Move!" to a mountain and it will fall into the sea. He isn't talking about mountains like the Alps. He is trying to tell us, here, that even just a little belief in God is enough to plow through huge problems.

Most of us come into recovery with a lot of fear. It is important to know that courage isn't the *absence* of fear. Courage is going forward anyway, *in spite* of fear. It means taking the next step, even though we are afraid. We all get afraid. There are over a hundred *fear not's* in the Bible because God knows we are fearful people. Fear only becomes a problem when we let it control our lives instead of confronting it with the truth of God's Word. Applying the principle of Chapter Two—recognizing that God IS and that He wants to help us—is the next step in healing and doing things differently.

Questions to Answer:

- List any experiences you've had that caused you to lose faith in God.

- What is keeping you from really believing that God can restore you to sanity?

- Describe times when God came through for you.

- List areas of your life you think God can't help you with.

- What do you remember being told as a child about God, faith, prayer, and forgiveness?

- Does your God have similar characteristics to your parents? For example, do you think of God as harsh, indifferent, distant, judgmental, unavailable, etc.?

- Do you have a punishing God who keeps score of your mistakes?

- Review the scriptures in this chapter that describe God's true nature. List what, in your reading, comforts and warms your heart about who God really is.

- Do you believe God hears your prayers? Do you believe God loves you?

- Do you realize you are not alone or unique?

- Do you believe you can love yourself and ask for help? Do you believe you don't have to do this alone?

- Can you believe that you have an inner strength that has gotten you to survive to this point?

- Can you believe there is hope for you?

- Do you believe that you are able to learn what you didn't learn, earlier in life, in order to become the person you were meant to be today?

Scriptures Related to Chapter Two:

Philippians 2:13   Psalms 34:18-20   Isaiah 40:29-31
2 Corinthians 1:9   John 3:16-17   Hebrews 11:1, 6
Mark 9:23-24

Prayer for Chapter Two:

Dear God,

Give me the faith to believe in You, that I may turn to You and receive Your love, protection, and care. Help me choose to walk in the ways that please You and bring peace. Amen.

THREE

Decision

Decide It: Make a decision to live and surrender
your life to God. *(Romans 12:1)*

Our third step in recovering our lives requires us to make a decision. First, we became aware of our condition, and then we
accepted the idea of God as a Power greater than ourselves. Now,
we decide to let God be completely in charge of our lives. We need
to let go of the tendency to analyze, question, and figure out the
problems in our minds. Surrender the thinking that tells you, "I
need to run my own show and make my own life happen." Even if
it seems difficult to let go and let God, the alternative is to ultimately face something worse. To follow God is to live. To turn from Him
is to die. Here in our third chapter, we decide if we want to live or
die. The more we let go and let God become the new manager of
our lives, the more we can live.

You may ask, "How do I trust in God's love when all I've ever
known is love that disappoints?" Or maybe you have trouble turning
your future over to Him for fear that He will make you do something
you don't want to do. After all, much of our past lives were spent
doing things we didn't want to do. It's important to learn about God's
goodness and about His love for us; otherwise, we'll continue to
project onto God expectations based on our earthly caretakers from
childhood, rather than on His true nature.

I personally struggled with the question, "Can I really trust God with my life?" After studying the Word regarding the nature of God, I reached the point where, intellectually, I could agree to surrender my life to His care, but emotionally, I still could not. My experiences had been so painful over the years, due to abuse and betrayal, that I could not feel comfortable trusting anyone, even God. I believed God was good, but emotionally I could not feel this nor could I overcome the fear that resulted from the "what if..." thinking that arose so often in my mind. What if I trust and surrender my will to God and things don't work out in my life? What if God doesn't come through for me? Then there would be nothing left to believe in or hope for. What if God's will for me is suffering? What if God's will for me is not what I want? Where would I go from there?

After some time in recovery, and after a lot of healing had taken place, I began dating Cap, a really good God-loving man. This was a first for me: a good relationship with a good man! Our relationship progressed in a very healthy way through the year. As it became apparent how we cared deeply for each other, he proposed marriage. I had always thought that was exactly what I wanted. Yet, when I was faced with this opportunity, I was overcome by fear. I was too afraid to say yes. I couldn't understand myself; he had not done anything to create such fear.

Two weeks after his proposal, I told my potential fiancée that my many painful experiences in life were making it hard for me to trust enough to accept his proposal. I told him how baffled I felt, given that, in the past, I'd said *yes* to other men I actually feared, yet now, I was saying *no* to someone I didn't fear at all. In my old life, I impulsively jumped into marriage with the wrong people and without any thought at all. Now, I was doing everything right *with* Mr. Right, and I couldn't say *yes* because I was scared to death! It made no sense!

For the next two weeks, I battled the fear of being hurt again. I argued with myself, telling myself that I had put my faith in God, and God had picked this partner for me. So what was there to be afraid of? Finally, I realized what my worst fear was: *What if it didn't work out this time, even though God had done the picking?*

Two weeks went by, and Cap and I continued to talk it out. I felt really stuck. One day, Cap said, "I believe I have the answer you're looking for." And he told me, "You don't have to be afraid of me doing something to hurt you. I wouldn't, because I'm afraid of your father," he said.

His answer confused me. My father had been one of my worst abusers, emotionally and mentally, so why did Cap think *his* fear of my father would ease my fear and comfort me? But Cap explained that he didn't mean my earthly father. It was my Heavenly Father he was afraid of, because he knew how much He loved me and that He wouldn't stand for anyone hurting His daughter.

When I heard Cap's explanation, weeks of fear instantly disappeared. I cried with relief. I suddenly knew I could trust this marriage because God was in the midst of it. I realized I could trust God with Cap. My fears had come from a place of trying to put my trust in Cap, not in God.

I know all too well that people are fallible. But when I entrust the people in my life to God, that act not only relieves my fears but also takes the pressure off others for being responsible for my serenity.

So I accepted Cap's proposal with joy and peace in my heart. We have enjoyed a solid, loving marriage that has lasted now for over twelve years. I have experienced untold blessings through our union. And to think I would have missed out on all of this if I hadn't applied our Chapter Three work—deciding to trust God—to my fears of Cap's proposal!

Today, when I question, "Can I trust my life to God?" all I have to do is think about what God did for us to show us how much He loves us, sending His only Son into the world so that we may be changed and live on through Him. This is real love. It is not that we loved God, but that He loved us and sent His Son as a sacrifice to take away our sins. (1 John 4:9-10)

Wouldn't it be nice if we could just trust God and feel the peace of not having to be in charge of everything? Wouldn't it be nice to not have to worry about our future? Surrendering our lives, as a way of life, reduces stress. Turning our lives over to God involves opening the door of our hearts to His love. Filling up on God's love helps us avoid the emotional relapses of feeling desperate and needy in a relationship. It helps us overcome our most powerful insecurities.

It is easier to surrender our lives to Christ when we take the time to learn about Him and why He came.

Who Is Jesus and Why Did He Come

God knew, even when He created man, that we would reject Him and fall out of His plan. So from the very beginning, God also put into effect a plan to save us from ourselves and restore us to Himself. When Adam was warned by God not to turn to evil, he didn't listen. Adam's disobedience, and his attempt to hide his truth from God, broke the perfect union between man and God. That act of disobedience defines human nature: We are literally born with an *earthly tendency to sin.*

God needed to reconcile the distance sin had created between man and God. His divine plan of redemption was to become a man, Himself, to repair the damage Adam had done. Part of the enormous mystery of God is His ability to be a three-in-one God: Himself as Father; Himself as Son; and Himself as Holy Spirit. It might help to understand that trinity by realizing that we, ourselves, have more than one identity. For instance, I am a wife, a mother, and a friend. I'm one person who relates to others from various aspects of my unified being. In just that way, Father, Son, and Holy Spirit are the three aspects of our loving God.

Jesus, as the Son of God, came to earth to fulfill all the laws of the Old Testament, under which humankind was condemned by Adam's sin. If Jesus had fallen into sin, as Adam had—if He had yielded to temptation and evil—He would have lost His authority over everything. This was the great risk.

But Christ overcame every temptation so that you and I could be free. Jesus did everything necessary to pay for our sins and restore us to God. He passed every faith test and every love test— to the point of sweating blood. He came to destroy the works of darkness, as we are told in 1 John 3:8. Jesus gave up His life as the price for our sins so that we could have forgiveness, restoration, and salvation. (Colossians 2:13-14)

Through that act, Jesus the man and Jesus as God made a new covenant. A covenant is a legally binding agreement between parties—in this case, God and us. And that covenant, made through Jesus, is that from here on out, no matter what, *we are God's own.* That covenant was made by God *with Himself.* We cannot change His covenant with Himself, no matter what we do.

Neither can we do a single thing to *earn* such forgiveness and love. There's no way we can get to Heaven through any of our own efforts. We can only receive and partake of God's love if we receive it as a gift. This covenant was sealed in God's Word—Jesus—and has to be kept for all time.

Try to imagine what it felt like for God to give up His only Son for each of us. Then try to imagine what it felt like to watch His only Son get beaten mercilessly to the point of death, all so that others even as yet unborn could live forever. Can you begin to conceive more deeply, more intimately, God's unimaginable love for you? Sit quietly and try to contemplate the unspeakable love God has for you and for every person.

Scripture tells us that Jesus was the first born of God and that He was born to show us that we, too, could become as children of God. He was the light to lead us out of the darkness. But it is only by having our own personal relationship with God that we *experience* the Bible and thereby become children of God.

Sin separates us from God. But turning to Jesus is the way in which God can become a Father to us, just as He is to Jesus. As our Father, God's commitment to us as His children is to forgive our past, protect us from future mistakes, create a new person within us, give us peace, and comfort our spirits.

God promises that if we seek Him, we will find Him. He promises us eternal life; He promises that our spirits will never die. He promises far more than what we could hope for or imagine. And all these promises are written in the Bible, His 'promise book' for us.

To know more about Jesus, you can turn to Scripture for descriptions of His nature and character, about how He feels toward us, how He looks at us, and what we were created for. Below are some of the names and roles by which Jesus is referred to in the Bible:

Jesus is the BRIDEGROOM and the head of His church (the body of believers). His church is the bride. (Mark 2:19-20)

Jesus is EMMANUEL, which means "God with us." Through him, God entered space and time to become one of us so we might be with God forever. (Matthew 1:23)

Jesus is GOD'S IMAGE, the perfect picture of God, because Christ and the Father are one. (Colossians 1:15)

Jesus is our SAVIOR. He seeks and saves the lost. (Matthew 1:21; 18:11; Acts 16:31)

Jesus is our JUDGE-RULER, as well as our advocate and lawyer, our defender before the bar of God's justice. (Romans 8:33-34)

Jesus is the LAMB OF GOD, our sacrificial lamb. His sacrifice paid for our sins, past, present, and future. (John 1:29; 1 Peter 1:18—19)

Jesus is the LIGHT OF THE WORLD; Jesus reveals truth. (John 8:12)

Jesus is THE WAY, THE TRUTH & THE LIFE. He is our path to God. He is the map, the road, the destination and the one who has gone ahead of us. (John 14:6)

Jesus is the PRINCE OF PEACE. Jesus bears our burdens and gives us rest. He has ended the conflict between God and man by His death on the cross. He also brings us an inner peace through the love of His spirit in our hearts. (Isaiah 9:6; Matthew 11:29-30)

Jesus is RESURRECTION AND THE LIFE. Death could not hold Him, nor can it hold any who are in Him. Jesus offers freedom not condemnation. Jesus *rids* us of what we *don't need* in our lives. (John 11:25; Romans 8:1- 2)

Jesus is UNLIMITED in POSSIBILITIES, and He always works for our *good*. (Romans 8:28; 1 Corinthians 2:9-10; Romans 4:17)

Jesus is FORGIVING. (Acts 13:38)

Jesus is the GREAT HEALER of ALL; He meets our every need. (Matthew 12:15; Luke 4:18-19)

Jesus is our PROTECTOR. (Psalm 16:5-8)

Is there proof that Jesus is the only Son of God? Jesus said He was the Messiah who had been foretold in Old Testament prophecy 400 years before His birth—and He fulfilled over 300 Biblical proph- ecies concerning the coming Messiah. I have heard it said, "The probability of Jesus' fulfilling even eight of the prophecies is 1 in 10 to the 17th power. The probability of His fulfilling forty-eight of them is a probability of 1 in 10 to the 157th power." Those seem to be impossible mathematical odds.

Further proof that Jesus rose from the dead comes from the lives of eye witnesses. After the resurrection, Jesus' disciples were trans- formed from common citizens into bold preachers. Once ordinary, common men suddenly were empowered to bravely face persecution for testifying about what they had seen and experienced. (Acts 4:13) When they were questioned, and even when they were threatened with death, they remained steadfast to their eyewitness testimonies: that Jesus had died and had then risen from the dead. Even James, Jesus's brother, who for a long time had not believed Jesus was the Messiah, became an apostle after the resurrection; he died a martyr's death for proclaiming his brother as Christ.

Why would someone die for a lie? For something they "just made up"?

Even more proof can be found in the many people who saw Jesus alive after they'd witnessed His death. His enemies and the Roman soldiers who executed Him were fully satisfied that He was in fact dead. But after three days, 500 people as individuals and in groups, over a period of forty days, saw and touched Jesus as He walked, ate, and preached.

An eye witness report is found in 1 Corinthians 15:3-8:

For I delivered to you first of all that which I also received: that Christ died for our sins according to the Scriptures, and that He was buried, and that He rose again the third day according to the Scriptures, and that He was seen by Cephas, then by the twelve. After that He was seen by over five-hundred brethren at once, of whom the greater part remain to the present, but some have fallen asleep. After that He was seen by James, then by all the apostles. Then last of all He was seen by me also, as by one born out of due time.

The resurrection is important because it proved that Jesus was divine and that everything He taught and claimed is true. It reveals Jesus' power over death and the new life He offers. Remember, when Jesus was speaking to His disciples, He was actually speaking to you and me today, too, and to our children and to our children's children. He was speaking to all the people of the past, present, and future. **Jesus is alive and well today, in spirit, just as He existed in the body 2,000 years ago.** *"Jesus Christ is the same yesterday, today, and forever."* (Hebrews 13:8)

Receiving Christ

Why turn to Christ? If you have been abused and you feel like damaged goods, know that God can take what the world calls trash and make it even better than something brand-new. God is in the business of restoration; He turns uselessness into usefulness. He is in the business of filling empty spaces; He makes whole whatever is incomplete.

Many of us think we are incomplete if we're not married, if we don't have a college degree or high school education, if we lack money, or we don't have children. But if you know who you are in Christ, you have absolutely everything you need for an abundant life. God/Christ will be your husband, brother, friend, teacher, and/ or counselor. In God, we are complete. The meaning of the word *complete* is: finished, perfected, assured, satisfied, and secured. Colossians 2:10 says, "*. . . and you are complete in Him, who is the head of all principality and power.*"

None of us is unique. We have all missed the mark and fallen short of the glory of God. (Romans 3:23) We do not have to let the sins of the past determine what we do in the future. No matter what you have done, you can come to God and receive His love and forgiveness.

God's *commitment* is to forgive our sins, even our worst sins. God made that covenant with us. A contract is legal and binding. A contract is not about "feelings." God's doesn't change His position toward you from day to day, based on how He "feels" about your behavior. It is a "done deal."

God will not break the covenant He made with Himself through Jesus. No matter how many times we fail, no matter what we are or aren't able to understand about God and Jesus, God extends His forgiveness through Christ and takes us back if we ask Him to. When we turn to Him, we make an exchange with Him: We give Him our sins and He gives us His glory. We give Him our poverty and He gives us His riches. We give Him our garbage and He gives us His goodness. God invites us into this covenanted exchange-agreement, wherein we bring nothing to the table and He gives us everything: His nature, His character, His goodness, and His promises. God does not come to condemn us, but to save us!

Your only choice, now, is to reject or to participate in the amazing Grace.

God has even provided for us after physical death. Most people fear death. But what if you knew you were going to a place of utterly magnificent beauty and love, forever? When we turn to God, He gives us eternal life. John 3:16 says, *"For God so loved the world that He gave His only begotten Son, that whoever believes in Him should not perish but have everlasting life."* God wants us to live with Him forever.

Try to recognize *God* as your real Father, and know that He will take care of you the way your parents were supposed to—but a thousand times better! (Matthew 23:9) Psalm 27:10 says, *"Although my father and my mother have forsaken me, yet the Lord will take me up [adopt me as His child]."* (AMP) We are spiritual orphans, but Jesus plainly tells us that God will be a Father to those who accept Him. God created us in His own image, to be the family He could lavish His love on. Just as with people we love, God can hardly wait to see us and be with us. Everything we had hoped for in an earthly Father, we can find in God.

So how do we receive Christ? The Bible says we can be born two times. We are born physically into the world once, and our second birth occurs when we accept Jesus, when we are born into God's spiritual Kingdom and are adopted by God. The word *adoption*, as it's used here, means that we are brought into the image and likeness of God. When you discover that God is present right here, right now, you'll come to see the whole world with a different set of eyes. Everyone is God's child, no matter what. It is when we realize this and His love for us that we are born again. We become true sons and daughters through His love for us. It is a spiritual birth.

A life made over by God's love brings victory from defeat, freedom from bondage, self-acceptance, confidence, and peace. The healing power of God can completely change your life. The only way you can stay lost to God is to reject Him. To be in covenant agreement means that you accept God's grace to save you, to heal you, and to transform you. And you simply come as you are!

God is a free gift. Not even being a good, sincere person could "earn" God's gift. Ephesians 2:8-9 tells us, *"For by grace you have been saved through faith, and that not of yourselves; it is the gift of God, not of works, lest anyone should boast."*

Let the person you have been, die. You don't have to be stuck in something you can't do anything about, now: the past. When you let God come into your life, He can give you a new outfit to wear. It may be a little big at first, but with time, you can grow into it. God is waiting to adopt you. If God can raise Jesus from the dead, He can change and heal you because His spirit exists inside you. (Romans 8:11)

Maybe you've fought with addictions, bad habits, and wrong attitudes you couldn't seem to change. God offers you hope. He can make you over from the inside out. Ezekiel 36:26 tells us, *"I will give you a new heart and put a new spirit within you; I will take the heart of stone out of your flesh and give you a heart of flesh."*

The reason we don't have peace and a full life is because of our separation from God. God wants us to experience His peace in our lives, the peace that passes all understanding! (Philippians 4:7, John 14:27) God is the answer. Jesus claimed to be God in John 10:30: *"I and My Father are one."* He tells us that He is the way, the truth, and the life. (John 14:6) The way to God is through the cross.

God doesn't force Himself on us. We are free to turn away from Him and go our own willful way, even though that causes separation from Him. Yet when we decide to turn to Him, Romans 10:9 tells us, *"... that if you confess with your mouth the Lord Jesus and believe in your heart that God has raised Him from the dead, you will be made whole."* To receive Christ into our hearts, we are to confess, repent, and invite.

So what does it mean to confess, repent, and invite? "Sin" means "to miss the mark," to be off-center, God being the center. Usually, we try to cover up our sin, which is perfectly silly, because, of course, God knows about it! Since God already knows our sins, confessing them to Him is for *our* benefit, not *His*. By confessing, we show God our willingness to own our mistakes and repent of them.

To repent means to turn from sin and commit to amending one's life. We can't repent of something we won't admit to. But when we do repent, we bring our dark sin into God's light, and, with His help, we stop repeating that behavior—we "forsake" it.

When believers refer to the blood that Jesus shed, we're reflecting on the astonishing fact that God allowed the life force of His Son's body to be beaten out of Him in the crucifixion as a spiritual payment of *ransom*! The *old* contract on our lives was made under the law, after Adam. But God ransomed us under His new covenant with Himself through Jesus' crucifixion and made that old contract null and void. The act of *inviting* Jesus, the spirit of God, back into our hearts and lives is the spiritual act of signing on the dotted line to be released from previous spiritual laws and brought directly under His love and Grace.

One of the most powerful things we can do is pray. Jesus was a man of prayer. With much prayer comes much power. And when we start seeing the power and results of prayer, our faith and practice of it will naturally grow. The first step is to reach out in faith with a simple prayer inviting Jesus into our life.

Ask yourself the following questions:

- Are you looking for the power of God to bring victory into your life over your struggles?

- Are you tired of repeating your mistakes?

- Do you want to let go of the guilt you feel over your past?

If you want in on God's world of blessing and protection, if you want to know what living under the umbrella of the Kingdom of Heaven is like, I invite you to pray and receive Christ into your heart. Maybe you've suffered through failed marriages, abuse, addiction, alcoholism, depression, an eating disorder, spiritual bankruptcy, and an out-of-control life. Maybe you are facing any one of these overwhelming challenges right now. Christ can comfort and lead you through to the other side of whatever you are dealing with. You have nothing to lose. You are risking nothing in exchange for the possibility of gaining everything. Wouldn't you want to trade shame for honor, fears and resentments for love and forgiveness, bondage for freedom, and darkness for light?

If you would like to receive Christ, you can choose to pray the prayer below, which is based on scripture, or you can use it as an example and pray with your own specific words in a quiet place:

> *Dear Jesus,*
>
> *I live in a broken world, and I am broken. I believe You died for me and paid the debt for my behavior. I invite You to come into my life and create in me a new heart and a new person. Cleanse me from all of my past.*
>
> *Thank You for the gift of Your spirit, for the freedom and the new life You offer. Thank You for the promise that I will enjoy eternal life with You in the family of God. I am grateful that I no longer have to fear death and the unknown. I will use this new life to learn about You and Your love, and for loving others.*
>
> *In Jesus's Holy Name. Amen.*

If you prayed this prayer, the Bible says you can expect a change of life and that you will be blessed every day, as described in Galatians 3:14: *"... that the blessing of Abraham might come upon the Gentiles in Christ Jesus, that we might receive the promise of the Spirit through faith."* We are promised the blessings of Abraham, as found in Genesis 22:16-18: *"... I swear by Myself, declares the* LORD, *that because you have done this and have not withheld your son, your only son, I will surely bless you and make your descendants as numerous as the stars in the sky and as the sand on the seashore. Your descendants will take possession of the cities of their enemies, and through your offspring all nations on earth will be blessed, because you have obeyed Me."*

The good news is, God loves you and has a plan for your life. He has prearranged circumstances and people so you can have victory and success through Him. Ephesians 2:10 says, *"For we are His workmanship, created in Christ Jesus for good works, which God prepared beforehand that we should walk in them."* This means that we are created in Christ Jesus and can live the good life.

Seek after God. God has a love that will not give up on you or anyone else. God will accept you no matter where you have been or what you have done—God knows everything about you. He's not interested in ritual or religiosity, but in a relationship with you. The moment you realize God loves and accepts you, and you choose to accept His love and a relationship, you will be completely transformed in every aspect of your life. When you give your hopes and dreams to a real, live God, who wants to reveal Himself to you, and when you let Him have His way, you will receive far more than you could ever imagine.

Your part is to keep the faith, to do the next right thing, and to hang in there. Walking with God is a process of becoming. It is learning to believe and receive the promises of God in our new life. This does not happen overnight. Growing into the new you takes time and practice at throwing off your old ways. Ephesians 4:22-24 says, *"You were taught, with regard to your former way of life, to put off your old self, which is being corrupted by its deceitful desires; to be made new in the attitude of your minds; and to put on the new self, created to be like God in true righteousness and holiness."*

When you choose to follow Jesus, you embark on a journey. You are now God's child by His covenant through faith. The presence of God dwells within you. Visit with Him daily, talk with Him, and listen for Him. As you learn to turn your life over to Him, as you choose to trust, listen to and do the will of God, you will receive from God more than your heart could imagine because of His promise to you. God will use everything in your life to form a deeper relationship with Him. You're on a journey where the final destination is eternal life with God in Heaven.

Christ as Husband

The Word refers to us, the believers, as the bride of Christ, and to Christ as our bridegroom. Consider letting God unfold his plan for you regarding a mate as you read the following letter:

On His Plan for Your Mate

Everyone longs to give themselves completely to someone . . . to have a deep, full relationship with another . . . to be loved thoroughly and exclusively. But God, to the Christian says, "No, not until you are satisfied and content and fulfilled with being loved by Me alone . . . with giving yourself totally, and unreservedly to Me . . . [with] having an intensely personal and unique relationship with Me, alone . . .

"I love you, my child, and until you discover that only in Me is your satisfaction to be found, you will not be capable of the perfect human relationship I have planned for you.

"I want you to stop planning, stop wishing, and allow Me to bring that person to you . . . You just keep learning and listening to the things I tell you . . . You must wait!

"Don't be anxious. Don't worry. Don't look around at the things others have received. Don't look at the things you think you want. Just keep looking off and away up to Me, or you will miss what I want to show you.

"And then, when you are ready, I'll surprise you with a love more wonderful than you would ever imagine. You see, until you are ready and until the one I have for you is ready . . . (I am working, even this minute to have you both ready at the same time) . . . until you are both satisfied exclusively with Me and the life I have planned and prepared for you, you won't be able to experience the love that exemplifies your relationship with Me . . . and this is perfect love.

"Dear one, I want you to have this wonderful love . . . I want you to see in the flesh a picture of your relationship with Me and to enjoy materially and concretely the everlasting union of beauty and perfection and love that I offer you with Myself. Know that I love you utterly. Believe it and be satisfied."

—Author Unknown

As we seek to receive Christ into our heart, and seek to fully love Him, we can consider Him to be our true first love and husband.

Practice surrendering your life to Him. Do you realize that Christ wants to take your relationship to the next level—to *forever*? If you'll make a commitment to Him, He'll be the kind of lover and husband you've looked for your whole life in the wrong men.

If you believe, and if through faith become His bride in your heart and mind, giving your love to Him first, He will use all that He has in this world to love and care for you. His presence will become so strong that soon the unseen will be visible to you.

Commit to Him. He's the right one. Jesus looks for a bride. He's tired of girlfriends dating Him only in their hour of need. He wants to be in a full-time, committed relationship with you, just like in marriage. Isaiah 54:5 tells us, *"For your maker is your husband, the Lord of hosts is His name . . ."*

The important thing is, it's not *what* you offer Him, but *who* you offer Him. He has everything except one thing: you! Give Him yourself. Jesus is still alive today. He is everything that God loved and esteemed. He is called the Son, the first born of all creation. Jesus is the whole purpose of God. Everything was created by Him and for Him, and in Him all things hold together. He is the beginning and the end of all things. (Colossians 1:15, 16-17) We accomplish the whole purpose of God in our lives when we abide in Him. (Colossians 2:9-10)

Philippians 4:19 reminds us not to worry, because God cares for all our needs. But whatever we put ahead of God, we lose anyway. Making God your first love gets you on the right road. Think about the promise found in Matthew 6:33: *"But seek first the kingdom of God and His righteousness, and all these things shall be added to you."*

God promises us a new life as He heals and renews our mind and emotions through His Spirit and His Word. He offers us hope, peace, honor, protection, and love in exchange for our past sins and misery. While there are thousands of promises in the Bible, there are a few key lifesaving promises God gives us and stands by. Contemplate **God's Promises for Well Women** listed in the back of this book.

Questions to Answer:

- What parts of your life are you unwilling to turn over to God? What prevents you from giving them up?

- What do you hope to experience as a result of your decision to surrender to God's will?

- Do you believe you have to earn God's love?

- Can you accept and receive God's love for free?

- Do you realize that the God that brought you to this point is still with you and will never abandon you?

- Do you realize that God is your actual parent and has been there for you all along?

- Do you believe that God hears your prayers?

- Can you ask God to be there for you, no matter what happens?

- Are you willing to do whatever it takes to heal, change, and grow?

- Can you begin by surrendering your self-criticism and self-destructive attitudes and behaviors?

- Are you willing to ask for help?

- Are you willing to make God the center and focus of your love life?

Scriptures Related to Chapter Three:

Romans 12:1	Matthew 26:39	Proverbs 16:3
Romans 10:9-10	Galatians 2:20	Jeremiah 29:11-14

Prayer for Chapter Three:

Dear God,

I surrender my entire life to You. I have made a mess of trying to run it myself. You take the whole thing and run it for me, according to Your will and plan. I trust You to shape, develop, and heal me so that I may find freedom from the prison of my past brokenness and pain. I pray that You will use my new life, filled with Your love, power, and care, as a testimony to help others know You. Amen.

Making Peace with Yourself...

Troubles are often the tools by which God
fashions us for better things.

— *H.W. Beecher*

The next four chapters are the part of the solution
in which we get a reality check on where we are,
let in God's light, position ourselves to receive
God's healing, and allow that to happen.

FOUR

Inventory

Inventory It: Make an inventory (an account) of the resentments and fears in your relationships over the course of your life, starting in childhood. (*Lamentations 3:40*)

This step forward involves fearlessly looking at how we got to where we are. It means taking into account (inventorying) what is present in our lives, just as a store inventories the items on its shelves. An inventory necessitates thorough and complete honesty so that we may see the obstacles that have prevented us from having healthy relationships and knowing who we are. This step helps us discover the root cause of our fears, resentments, and challenges in relationships.

Until I did the work in this chapter, I remained a victim to my circumstances, always putting the blame on others for what happened to me in relationships. One day, when I was angry about how a man had treated me, my mentor had me write down exactly what he had done to make me so angry. I wrote that he had beaten up on me; that he hadn't been there for me; that he didn't listen to me; and that he criticized me constantly. I was particularly angry because, when he first met me, he seemed incapable of doing such things and, instead, had come across as very kind, loving, and considerate. I felt misled and deceived. He neglected me, closed himself off from me, and threatened to beat me when I got upset about anything he did. I had stayed with him because I was totally focused on wanting him to change to accommodate my needs and wants.

Looking over this paragraph with me, my mentor asked if I had ever treated myself the way that man had treated me?

Suddenly it became clear that, when I was with this man, *I* did not take responsibility for *myself*, for my needs or my desires in the relationship. *I* was not responding to *myself*, and that the man had merely mirrored exactly how I was treating myself. My denial, my unwillingness to see my part in the situation (in choosing and staying in the relationship), kept me from recognizing that it was **I** who had caused the disappointments in my adult life. I had volunteered to be the victim all along. For as long as I blamed others for the problems in my life, the pattern would continuously repeat itself. What the men in my life did was wrong, but if I didn't deal with my part in it, I would stay stuck and would most likely repeat the relationship pattern.

Seeing my part in perpetuating the pattern gave me a great sense of freedom. Suddenly, I viewed this man as a life lesson; a mirror in which I could see the truth about myself and set myself free. All the things he failed to do for me were the very things I needed to do for myself.

My question then changed from, "Why did he act this way to me?" to, "What can I learn from what happened?" By focusing on changing myself, which *was* possible, instead of on changing someone else, which is *not* possible, I could change my life and grow.

Denial is when we pretend that something does not exist when it really does. It is when we minimize the severity of a serious problem. When we blame others, justify (explain away), and make excuses for our behaviors (or someone else's), we are in denial. Getting mad and attacking back is just another form of denial, since even that keeps us from facing reality. It keeps us traveling on a downward spiral of abusive relationships and negative behaviors. As we put events down on paper and look at what has happened, we can actually *see*, in writing, the common thread or repeating patterns of behavior.

When stores take inventories, the managers identify what they have on their shelves. They need to know which items to keep and which are damaged or discontinued goods. Doing an inventory requires us to "take stock" of our fears, resentments, and our character defects and assets in relation to the people and situations in our lives. Here, we write honestly and simply—without trying to analyze or judge ourselves or our past behaviors. We do not have to figure anything out here; all we need to do is just write the list. God is with us on this journey as we write out our inventories.

Inventory of Resentments of People and Situations

The past can take a toll on us. If we are to live with serenity and peace, we have to let go of resentments we carry with us from our past. The authentic, useful feeling of real anger only lasts about five seconds. Beyond that point, we must nurture and "feed" the anger—and that is resentment, and it is part of what keeps us sick. Our spiritual unrest can close us off from God's light and truth. The exercise in this chapter is not meant to dwell and dredge up the past, but to identify our resentments so that we can let them go.

Resentments affect the way we think, feel, and behave, and they contribute to lowered self-esteem, diminished goals, and relationship difficulties. Taking a Resentment Inventory will help you examine situations in which resentment is a problem for you.

In this exercise, you look at the people and situations with whom you are angry. In the first column, list the people who hurt you, lied to you, cheated on you, etc.—anyone toward whom you feel resentments. List anyone or anything that bothers you.

The following is a list of types of people and relationships we might have resentments toward. Review the list to bring to mind any residual anger you may be carrying from the past or present:

Acquaintances   Friends

Aunts/Uncles   Father (Step-Father)

Boyfriends/Girlfriends   Grandfather/Grandmother

Brothers (Step-Brothers)	In-Laws
Sisters (Step-Sisters)	Lovers
Church	Clergy Mistress/Other
Woman	Mother (Step-Mother)
Co-Workers	Neighbors
Creditors	Police
Drug Dealers	Probation Officers
Doctors	Prostitutes
Ex-spouses	Salespeople
Spouse	Teachers

In the next column, write down what that person or relationship did that injured or upset you. You only need to need to write down resentments that are with you currently, not issues you've already dealt with and feel resolved about. Write honestly and keep it brief. Don't write more than fifteen to twenty words on any resentment.

We need to realize that the people who have harmed and wronged us were spiritually sick, too. As we journey through this process, we ask God to give us the patience, tolerance, and understanding we would like to receive from others. How many abusers were themselves abused? How many neglectful parents grew up as neglected children? Consider praying for the people who have wounded you as you would pray for any sick friend. Praying for them daily for a few weeks will help ease the sting of their treatment of you, and heal our own heart, as well.

In the third column of your Inventory, check the appropriate boxes indicating whether the wrong done to you affected your confidence, your dreams and hopes, your finances, your emotional stability, your home life, your family, or your friends.

Finally, in the fourth column, look for your part in whatever the situation is or was. Resentments are really anger recycled. They are an effort to shift the blame or guilt for our own part or participation in an event onto someone else. Coming out of an abusive relationship can leave us feeling victimized; making it hard to figure out where we have been at fault. In this last column, we look for our part in all our problem relationships. We need to put out of our mind the wrongs others have done to us, and look instead for our own mistakes that contributed to the harm we experienced. You may say, "No matter what I have done, it is always wrong for someone to be abusive or violent to someone else." This is true. Our part in an abusive relationship may be just and only not telling our abuser, "This relationship or behavior has to end" and then moving ourselves out of harm's way. Perhaps we thought it was loving to stay in a bad situation, not realizing that our doing so was actually hurting the other person by allowing them to act out of their sickness. That kind of tolerance actually causes harm to everyone.

Inventorying our resentments, finding the part we played in allowing the injuries we have listed, is the beginning of finding our way out of anger and other negative emotions. It can be difficult to discover what we did to contribute to the pain and wrongdoing we suffered. But there are various character traits we can look at— behaviors we learned from neglectful caretakers—that will help us identify our own blind spots. Our blind spots are what led us into the situations we have now listed in our inventory of resentments. When we can name those blind spots, we can develop new behaviors to prevent ourselves from re-engaging with the kinds of people and situations that can only bring us continued harm and damage.

Being a victim can mean: believing we had no choice in our situation; not removing ourselves from harm; not setting healthy boundaries to protect ourselves; sacrificing ourselves to please others; trying to fix or rescue people who don't want help; remaining in instability and chaos; staying silent at all costs; stuffing our feelings; taking on more responsibility than we can handle; telling white lies to cover up our home life. Those are just some of the ways we can unknowingly play a part in contributing to the abuse we suffer.

Resentment Inventory of People and Situations

I'm Resentful At	The Cause
List people and situations that made you angry:	Briefly note what happened and why you are angry:

What Felt Threatened?							My Part In It									
Check each area of your life that felt threatened from it:							Check which ones you had: **Character Defects**				Check which ones you had acted on: **Specific Behaviors**					
Confidence	Dreams & Hopes	Finances	Emotional Stability	Home Life	Family	Friends	Selfish	Self-Seeking	Dishonest	Fearful	Feeling Unworthy	People Pleasing	Being a Victim	Fixing Others	Fear of Abandonment	Impulsive Acts

For each resentment in this fourth column, check for any of the following four main character defects that describe your part in the injury you experienced. Were you:

SELFISH   (wanting what you want the way you wanted it).

SELF-SEEKING   (seeking only to further your own means/purpose with no consideration for another).

DISHONEST   (lying to yourself or withholding the truth from others).

FEARFUL   (afraid of being found out, not getting what you want, or losing what you have).

Look over the following list of specific, unhealthy patterns that may have contributed to your part in the injuries in your life. Then, going back to your final column in your inventory of resentments, check off the behavior patterns that describe your part in the situations on your list.

FEELING UNWORTHY. This relates to feelings of low self-esteem and inadequacy; judging and beating up on ourselves as a result of constant criticism, and often putting ourselves and our needs on a back burner. We were never encouraged to believe in our own abilities. We believed we were "bad" and the cause of our family problems, so we aimed at being perfect to avoid painful criticism. But no matter how hard we tried, we could never please the adults in our life. Our lack of self-esteem made us fearful of making mistakes and taking risks. We felt overly responsible for things that went wrong, and learned not to accept credit when something went right. We lived in anticipation, always waiting for the other shoe to drop. We were nonassertive, fearful of failure and rejection, and had a negative self-image.

PEOPLE PLEASING. We wanted people to like us, so we said *yes* when we wanted to say *no.* We changed who we were so that we wouldn't lose a relationship. We sought validation from others because we didn't know how to give it to ourselves. Fearing disapproval and criticism from others, we looked for love in all the wrong places. We put aside our own wants and needs, feelings and desires, in order to avoid hurting the other person in a destructive relationship. We lost ourselves by not being true to ourselves or expressing ourselves for fear of displeasing someone else. Often, we feared disagreeing with someone, fearing the retaliation we would suffer for speaking up.

BEING A VICTIM. We felt trapped, vulnerable, and hopeless to get out of crisis and chaos. Not knowing how to exercise choice, we did not set and enforce healthy boundaries by taking ourselves out of harm's way. Feeling responsible for another's feelings and personal challenges, we had difficulty separating from toxic unhealthy relationships.

FIXING OTHERS. We often chose to love people we thought we could rescue, and spend most of our time dealing with other peoples' problems in order to avoid looking at ourselves. We often confused love with pity. The more chaotic the situation, the more indispensable we felt. We tried to control and change other people by fixing them, thinking that, by doing so, we could determine the outcome of events. We have an exaggerated sense of responsibility, which causes us to take on far more than we can handle effectively. We often end up feeling victimized, abused, unappreciated, and resentful of taking on responsibilities for others (even while offering to do so!). We keep trying to control outcomes of unpredictable events. We are unavailable to ourselves.

FEARING ABANDONMENT. This driving fear causes us to deny, minimize, or repress our feelings about a harmful situation or relationship. We stay in the relationship because we are terrified of losing it. We often choose partners who are emotionally unavailable or addicted, yet we try to get them to meet our needs. To that end, we try to please those partners and to meet their needs in hopes of reducing the possibility of abandonment. The drive to avoid abandonment takes priority over honestly confronting relationship issues or conflicts.

BEING IMPULSIVE. We act before thinking and let our feelings dictate and direct our actions instead of waiting for God's lead and guidance. We settle for less than what we want by doing things without thought and by making commitments we regret later.

ISOLATING. If we are keeping secrets about how abusive our relationship is — or if we feel ashamed because we think we "cause" our abuse — we often feel uneasy being around other people. We withdraw to feel safe, to keep our secrets from being found out, and to avoid having to confront the truth about a situation we need to either change or leave.

Once you have filled in all four columns of the Resentment Inventory, you will see very clearly, reading from left to right:

the resentment (column 1)
the cause (column 2)
the part of self that has been affected (column 3)
and the defects/behaviors that allowed the abusive relationship/
    situation (column 4)

Now look at the following two areas in your Resentment Inventory:

- Look for things that happened in the past or present that didn't go your way.

- Then go to "What is your part in it."

After you finish reviewing your resentment inventory, answer the following questions:

- What are your major weaknesses? How did they hurt you?

- What current behavior is most damaging to your life?

- What do you think you are in denial about?

Fear of People and Situation Inventory

Fear stems from self-pity, self-seeking, selfishness, and self-centeredness. It is often rooted in thoughts of either, "What if I lose something that I have?" or "What if I don't get something that I want?"

Many of us live with a thousand forms of fear. Fear is a destructive fiber that can get woven through every aspect of our lives. If not dealt with, it can influence our thinking and lead us on a downward spiritual spiral. Taking a Fear Inventory moves us from being afraid of something, to learning how to discern the difference between reasonable and unreasonable concerns. Fear will activate our character defects and self-destructive behaviors. Fear can hinder our ability to perceive God's guidance, and cause us to make choices that can hurt us and others. A good Fear Inventory can help us see where we are self-reliant and need to become God-reliant in our thoughts and actions.

This inventory will help you examine situations in which fear creates problems for you. Completely fill out Column 1, from top to bottom, before going on to Column 2, where you will write down why you have the fear. Again, complete Column 2 from top to bottom before going on to Column 3.

In Column 3, we look for the connection between our fear and our self-will and self-reliance. In Column 4, we identify a corresponding promise of God's that can dispel the fear. Complete Column 3 and Column 4 at the same time for each fear entry.

Before you begin writing your Fear Inventory list, it might be useful to look over the list below of examples of fear. This might help you recall more of your own fears.

Fear of abandonment	Fear of intimacy
Fear of authority	Fear of judgment
Fear of being alone	Fear of living
Fear of being found out	Fear of loneliness
Fear of being hurt	Fear of losing control
Fear of change	Fear of losing a person you love
Fear of condemnation	Fear of losing something you have
Fear of confrontation	Fear of men
Fear of disapproval	Fear of not getting what you want
Fear of dying	Fear of parents
Fear of emotions	Fear of people
Fear of failure	Fear of rejection
Fear of family	Fear of relapse
Fear of fear	Fear of responsibility
Fear of receiving	Fear of self-expression
Fear of God	Fear of sex
Fear of hurting others	Fear of success
Fear of insanity	Fear of the unknown
Fear of insecurity	Fear of unemployment

With these examples of fear in mind continue on and fill out the following Fear Inventory of People and Situations.

Fear Inventory of People and Situations

List People and Situations that you Fear:	What do you Fear Will Happen:	Where is your Trust and Reliance?		What does God Promise: (Find a promise of God to replace the fear)
		God	Self	

Look at your list. Are you *afraid* you're not good enough, *afraid* you won't measure up, *afraid* of being hurt, *afraid* of what will happen, *afraid* of what won't happen, *afraid* of your feelings, *afraid* of being blamed, *afraid* of being responsible, *afraid* of what someone will do, *afraid* of what you will do? Ultimately, we're *afraid* of not being loved and we're afraid of being left and abandoned. Ask yourself:

- Are you *afraid* of almost everything?

- Why are you so *afraid*?

Look at how fear and self-reliance feed your shortcomings. Can you see that your fear of not being loved and your fear of being abandoned have contributed to being in an unhealthy relationship/situation? Can you begin to choose to trust and rely on God, instead of on yourself?

When we are in fear, we are looking at life through the lens of self-reliance. We have cut God out of the equation. We are usually considering a situation, a relationship, or a challenge solely on the basis of our own limited abilities to deal with or create it. When we think and feel that we are alone in dealing with life on life's terms, life is indeed a fearful place.

The key to dispelling fear and living in faith is to invite God back into the equation. We need to become God-reliant, instead of self-reliant, to restore our faith and dispel our fear. When fear overwhelms us, we can choose to change our mindset and perspective; to reaffirm and claim God's promises to provide for, to protect us and to meet our every need. And when we are in a difficult challenging situation or relationship, we can remember that He promises to never abandon us, to walk with us through whatever we are facing. Finally, we can focus and rely on God's promise of a victorious outcome in the end, His promise to turn into good what was meant for harm in our life.

The time spent living between identifying the challenge and experiencing the outcome is the time to develop, strengthen, and walk in faith. This is the time to practice focusing on the promise and not the problem. We may not yet feel or experience the promise, but we can keep refocusing our attention on it. Eventually, fear will leave and faith will follow.

Every time fear crops up in your experience, identify it and immediately choose to view the problem through God's eyes, reminding yourself to live a God-reliant life, rather than in a limited self-reliant life. You can apply this principle to every fear you experience.

To begin with, we often fear what we have no control over. And rarely can we figure out what God is doing on the front end. So why not just seek God's will, asking what He wants you to **be** and **do**. When you choose to let God handle and direct what overwhelms and frightens you, you begin to get a sense that you really do have what you need to handle the situations and people in your life; you no longer need to fear them.

Once you have completed your Fear Inventory, go back through each fear and say the following prayer: *God please remove this fear and show me what you want me to be and think.*

In our Chapter Four recovery work, we are seeking to let go of resentments and move through our fears. We are looking for protection from harm and for the peace that comes with safety. Your greatest safety is in God. Draw close to Him and He will protect you in ways beyond your understanding. Read Psalm 91:1-15 each morning and night, and meditate on what God is telling you in it. You can recite it in its entirety or choose specific parts of it to repeat throughout the day:

> *He who dwells in the secret place of the Most High*
> *Shall abide under the shadow of the Almighty.*
> *I will say of the LORD, "He is my refuge and my fortress;*
> *My God, in Him I will trust."*
> *Surely He shall deliver you from the snare of the fowler*
> *And from the perilous pestilence.*
> *He shall cover you with His feathers,*

And under His wings you shall take refuge;
His truth shall be your shield and buckler.
You shall not be afraid of the terror by night,
Nor of the arrow that flies by day,
Nor of the pestilence that walks in darkness,
Nor of the destruction that lays waste at noonday.
A thousand may fall at your side,
And ten thousand at your right hand;
But it shall not come near you.
Only with your eyes shall you look,
And see the reward of the wicked.
Because you have made the LORD, who is my refuge,
Even the Most High, your dwelling place,
No evil shall befall you,
Nor shall any plague come near your dwelling;
For He shall give His angels charge over you,
To keep you in all your ways.
In their hands they shall bear you up,
Lest you dash your foot against a stone.
You shall tread upon the lion and the cobra,
The young lion and the serpent you shall trample underfoot.
Because he has set his love upon Me, therefore I will deliver him;
I will set him on high, because he has known My name.
He shall call upon Me, and I will answer him;
I will be with him in trouble;
I will deliver him and honor him.

Recognizing a Predator

Many of us have residual resentment and fears from the unhealthy and abusive relationships we put ourselves in, as adults, and stayed in. We either didn't recognize the predatory characteristics of an abusive mate early enough, or, once involved, we didn't know how to leave the relationship.

As we come out of denial and take responsibility for our lives and choices, we need to learn to listen to our intuition, our gut instincts, when they signal something is wrong. Often, that intuition is God's inner voice, red flags warning us to turn away.

The truth is, hurting people hurt others. If you were raised by neglectful or abusive parents, you can understand that another wounded person's behavior has its roots in his own painful childhood. You can understand their inability to be there for you. Parents who are hurt, themselves, and are hiding from their own pain, don't always know how to be there for their children.

Healing comes from dispelling denial, seeking the truth, and not staying a victim while hoping others will change to make us okay. But the truth will set us free. When we face the truth, we are able to see that we are valuable, wonderful, and lovable, even though we made mistakes. When we can spot our part in the problem, we become empowered because we can change ourselves. As we grow, we heal ourselves so that, one day, we can establish relationships built on present truths, not reenactments of the past.

So how do we recognize a potentially abusive man early on? Some men are predators who prey on needy, wounded women. A predator stalks the prey and then he pounces. A predator usually doesn't appeal to your fear, because that would scare you away. He appeals to your sympathy and looks to find your soft spot, your places of weakness and vulnerability. He figures out your doubts and insecurities, and sometimes even acts as if he feels them, too. Over time, as he wears down your defenses, you let your guard down because you're walking around with a big, uncomfortable void in your life—the void that comes from growing up with addiction, alcoholism, abuse, neglect, abandonment, or an absentee parent. As the predator tries to fill the emptiness in you, you think it is love. At first, anyway, it seems as if it is. The problem is, he also has a similar void in his life, and he begins to feed off you to fill his own emptiness. Your void becomes bigger and bigger as he feeds off you, which only makes you needier. Your self-esteem continues to be whittled away, and a downward spiral ensues. You can't fill a void with another void. You can only fill it with God.

This describes the general dynamics of abusive relationships.

In the end, when the relationship self-destructs, we are left empty, drained, and used up. The way to stop repeating that kind of relationship is to invest the time, focus, and energy needed to partner with God in our healing, and by saying *no* to abusive people and *yes* to ourselves. A predator can't have any power over us unless we give it to them.

Learning what real love is prevents you from being fooled by predatory men. Know that talk is cheap and actions speak louder than words. Wait and watch what a person does over time. It will prove out their character and integrity. Don't jump into bed with just anybody. You have a right to protect yourself, and you need to confront conscienceless behavior. A predator doesn't want to be held accountable for his actions. If, when confronted, your man dodges and defends his actions, consider it a warning sign. And if he gets mad and blames you, consider it a double red flag. A healthy relationship means that two people can confront even very difficult matters, discuss them maturely, and take responsibility for themselves.

Scriptures Related to Chapter Four:

Lamentations 3:40	James 1:19-21	Ephesians 4:31
Psalms 139:23-24	1 John 4:18	Colossians 3:5, 7-10

Prayer for Chapter Four:

Dear God,

Help me have tolerance, patience, and kindness toward those who have offended me. Keep me from feeding my anger and teach me to pray for those who have hurt me as I seek Your will for my life. Remove my fear, and guide me in what You would have me be and do.

Mold me after Your ideals and standards, and help me live up to them. I pray for Your guidance to do the next right thing in each situation, that I may live in sanity, health, love, and peace. Amen.

FIVE

Telling It

Tell It: Tell God, yourself, and someone else all about you and your inventory. *(James 5:16a)*

In Chapter Five, we look at the honesty required to confess and admit our part in the wrongdoings we have experienced in our lives. We will learn why we need to make this admission to God, to ourselves, and to another person. When we do this work, we set aside our pride and see ourselves as we really are. We trust God to give us the courage to look at ourselves, to express our truths, and to accept who we are. Through "telling it," we can let go of old ways of surviving and move on to new and healthier lives.

But before we go further, we need to discuss a problem many of us suffer from. It is called codependency, and you have no doubt discovered, in making your inventories, that codependency has been a major issue, both in relationships and within yourself.

A *codependent* person uses relationships to avoid dealing with his or her own life. This dependence parallels the disease in which addicts and alcoholics discover that a substance controls their choices and behaviors. Codependents are addicted to other people. They focus more on the person they're in relationship with than on their own lives. Driven by an addiction to love, some of us got into, or stayed in, hurtful and abusive situations because we were too focused on gaining love, approval, and self-esteem from sources outside of ourselves. We became (co)dependent on someone else to fulfill our needs, and in the process, we lost ourselves.

Loss of self through codependence is the cause of many of the character defects and dysfunctional behavior patterns now rooted in our relationships and lives. If the adults in our lives were out of control and caused us deep sorrow and disappointment, we grow up afraid to let others be who they are for fear that they will cause us more sorrow and disappointment. We fear letting life unfold naturally. Early-life experiences taught us to try to control people and events, and we do so by using helplessness, guilt, coercion, threats, advice-giving, manipulation, or domination. Unfortunately, our efforts usually either fail or they provoke anger in others.

As victims and codependents, we tend to either ignore problems or pretend they aren't happening. This, as we've learned, is denial. We pretend circumstances aren't as bad as they are, and we tell ourselves that things will be better tomorrow. We watch as problems get worse; we believe lies; we lie to ourselves; and we wonder why we feel as if we are going crazy. Lacking feelings of happiness, contentment, and peace within, we look to others to supply those feelings for us, and we feel terribly threatened by the possibility of losing the person we think provides our happiness.

As victims and codependents, we tend to think everything is our fault, and we believe our opinions don't matter. We wait to express our feelings until we know what other peoples' opinions are, and then we agree with them. In that respect, we are like chameleons. We have a difficult time standing up for ourselves and an even harder time expressing our emotions honestly, openly, and appropriately. We think most of what we have to say is unimportant, and we apologize for bothering people. We often talk in critical, self-degrading ways about ourselves. We frequently allow other people to hurt us.

Part of getting free of the awful traps inherent in codependency involves doing the exercises found here in Chapter Five. It is not a comfortable process, yet through this rough process of confessing our fears and resentments, we become more aware of and can move out of the painful survival behaviors we learned early in life. I invite you here to take a breath of courage and commitment and then read on.

When we took our inventories in Chapter Four, we exposed our feelings, memories, character defects, unhealthy behaviors, resentments, fears, and relationship harms. By looking at our part in our painful relationships, we gained hope for change, growth, and healing. Telling It, in Chapter Five, puts an end to isolating from others, feeling unique, and being alone.

We begin with the least threatening part of this step: admitting our wrongs to ourselves. This helps us come out of the denial and self-deception that has allowed us to see only what we have wanted to see. Confessing our truths to ourselves prepares us for our conversation with God and then with another human being.

To talk to yourself, you might try standing in front of a mirror. As you speak, try to view yourself as though your reflection were another person. Say out loud to yourself what you wrote in your Resentment Inventory and your Fear Inventory. Listen to what you are saying. Take note of any deeper understanding that you come up with in this exercise.

Next, we "step it up" a bit and tell it all to God—and we do this for our own sake, not God's. He already knows what we are finally willing to tell Him. In saying these things to God, we are repeating them to ourselves, as well—but now, there is something different: Now, by admitting our truths to God, we are also agreeing to take responsibility for them. *I* did these things; *I* had these thoughts and feelings. No more blame game. *I* am ready to change my behaviors, thoughts, and feelings. This takes great courage, but it also gives us a chance to experience how much God loves us and to realize that He has been waiting for us to admit our wrongs and to learn from our past behaviors.

To make yourself more conscious of God, try sitting across from an empty chair and imagine that God is sitting in that chair. Speak out loud, sincerely and honestly sharing your understanding of the insights you gained from your Chapter Four inventories. This can be a powerful, cleansing experience, and deep emotions may surface as a result of it.

You can start with a simple prayer such as:

God, I understand that You already know me completely. I am now ready to humbly admit to You my resentments and fears, my part in my behaviors and relationships, and my character traits. I'm grateful You have brought me to this point in my life. Take away my fear that You will reject me for revealing myself. I put myself and my life in Your care. Amen.

Begin with your Resentment Inventory. Share all aspects of it. Then go over your Fear Inventory. Finally, share any insights about yourself that you have gained. Finish with a prayer of thanks, and ask for the Holy Spirit to fill you. For example:

Holy Spirit, Release Your loving spirit and grace me with Your presence. God, give me the willingness to seek You and turn to You. Help me surrender my life to You. Fill me with your Holy Spirit; teach and guide me that I may better do Your will. Amen.

The third and final part of Step Five is confessing your wrongs to another person. The two-way nature of this encounter is a vital part of our process of self-revelation. Carefully choose the person who will be your listener. Pick someone who understands what you are trying to do and who will not try to change your plan. Since it is difficult to admit our mistakes to another person, choose someone you're comfortable with and trust to keep your confidence. If you have deep-rooted trust issues, you can pick a minister, a doctor, a therapist, or a psychologist, people who are legally bound to keep confidentiality. You may also choose to share your story with a member of a recovery program or a trusted friend (of the same sex).

When you meet with the person you have chosen, begin with prayer, asking God to be present. Ask Him to guide and support you as you go through the work of sharing your truths. Finally, ask

God to give you insights in this process of confessing your truths to another person.

Begin by sharing your resentments, then your fears. It is not necessary to discuss how the wrongs came about or how changes will be made. You are not seeking advice; you are simply telling another person what has gone on and is going on presently.

(If you are a listener to another person's inventories, be patient, receptive, and non-judgmental. You are God's representative and your job is to communicate unconditional acceptance. You are there to help the other person express her thoughts clearly. Ask questions, when necessary, so that the information is clearly understood by both of you. When this work is completed, both people can share their feelings about the whole experience. It is now possible to extend love to each other the way God gives love to each of us individually. Observe confidentiality.)

Let me tell you about my own experience with this process. Before I did this work, I carried so much shame about my life that eventually I had a nervous breakdown. I didn't think I could bear all my feelings anymore. I was desperate for help. All the thinking, analyzing, and intellectualizing I'd done in recent years had only helped me to survive—not to heal, grow, and change. My breakdown happened just as I was about to work this Telling It step, so I brought my assignment with me to the local mental hospital I checked into.

After my initial intake session with a nurse, she and the doctor tagged me with suicidal ideations and put me in a room where I would be monitored. They went through my suitcase and took away my razors, belts, and mirrors. I was relieved to be there, and I was committed to doing whatever they asked of me. I was ready to face myself head on. I was scared, but "the next step," whatever that proved to be, was my only hope.

I decided not to wait for "a better time" to do my Telling It assignment, but to do it right there in my hospital room. I was willing to do whatever it took to get better. My first evening in the hospital, unable to sleep, I took out my list of all my fears and resentments—the inventory of what was inside me. My mentor had suggested to me exactly what I have just suggested to you: that I should speak my list right out loud, first to myself in a mirror, then to God in a chair, and finally to another human being.

Holding my list, I stood before a fake, plastic mirror and began reading out loud all that was on the list. As I was doing so, a nurse opened the door and saw me talking to myself in the mirror. Startled, and knowing what this must look like, I turned to explain. But she just quickly excused herself and left, shutting the door behind her. That felt uncomfortable. I wasn't crazy, just depressed. But it wasn't the first time I'd been misunderstood, so I finished in front of the mirror, and then continued with the next exercise.

I put a chair next to my bed for God, and I sat on my bed and began reading my life out loud to Him. Halfway through the exercise, I began to imagine God *really* sitting in front of me. The door opened and, again, the nurse eyed me as I sat talking to an empty chair. Again, I began to explain that this was not what it looked like, but she motioned that it was okay and shut the door behind her again.

When I had initially questioned my mentor about the necessity for talking to the mirror and to God in an empty chair, she had reminded me of the story in the Bible about a man who asked a prophet to heal his leprosy. The man of God told him to wash in the pool seven times, after which he would be healed. The sick man questioned the logic of doing this, but when he did what he was told, he was instantly healed. (Mark 1:40-42) I was told that humility is knowing you are not God; knowing that, instead, you *need* God and that He's in charge. Humility is knowing what you can and cannot do and being humble enough to accept that. There are times when God requires us to do things that challenge our intellect and logic; but God knows that we need to stretch our faith and practice His ways.

Therefore, I followed directions, regardless of what I looked like, and when I finished the exercise, I did feel some peace. Over the next two weeks, I was treated for Post-Traumatic Stress Disorder

(PTSD), a dis-ease that affects people who were victims of traumatic events, most commonly people who grew up in dysfunctional or neglectful homes, or war veterans.

Each day, I participated in intensive group therapy aimed at helping me go back to the most frightening and damaging experiences in my life, mainly in my childhood. As I relived each episode, I re-experienced the deeply suppressed emotions I had been too afraid to feel when they occurred. Sometimes, I was so frightened that I wanted to run out of the hospital, but fortunately, I was locked in.

The staff helped me express and release a lot of pent-up rage. They encouraged me to use a plastic bat and hit a picture I had drawn of the face of the molester. After I swung the bat a few times, a rage pulsed through me and I let out a guttural cry so loud, it rang through all the halls of that hospital ward. I collapsed on the floor with the doctors and nurses holding onto me. All the violations of all the men in my childhood, all the criticism, all the rage directed at me by my father, all the countless injustices I had swallowed and stuffed as a child—all of that came pouring out of me.

In the hospital, I experienced my emotions in front of and with other people, thus ending the decades of silence and isolation. The other patients honored me by opening and baring their souls to me, in turn. We shared honestly what we had felt and believed about ourselves, our deep, dark secrets, our pains and fears. Together, we helped each other heal a little bit more. I kept thinking, "Our secrets keep us sick." Conversely, bringing our secrets into the light moves us deeper into freedom and healing.

The last part of my assignment, like yours, was to find another person with whom to disclose the secrets I had kept hidden all my life and that had kept me in shame and guilt. This was to be different from the sharing I had done in the hospital, where I talked for the first time about *things others had done to me when I was a powerless child*. Now, it was time to talk with someone about my part in the difficulties I had experienced in the *rest* of my life. Since I didn't yet know anyone I trusted enough to share those things with, I found someone who was legally bound to keep information confidential: a pastor.

I met with him and I told him everything. I told him that I had stolen, drunk, drugged, lied, had an affair, and that I had committed murder in the form of having an abortion in my early twenties. Stopping the life of that unborn child was one of my biggest regrets. In short, I shared all the deep, dark secrets I had carried for many years. As I reviewed them in front of the pastor, I realized I had broken every commandment God had given. I began to weep.

The minister explained that no one can follow the commandments without God's grace. The purpose of the commandments is to show us how totally we depend on *God's* strength, not our own. I had always assumed I could never measure up to what God wanted me to be, and the minister's input helped me understand that I was right: God actually understood all my weaknesses and wanted me to know how incapable of right living I was without Him. I knew I was nothing without God. I had proved that well in my life.

After completing my Chapter Five work of confession, I felt relieved and lighter. I felt a tingling from head to toe. Miraculously, I began to feel better. Something had begun to fill that hollow space inside me. Something felt a little more connected, more real inside me. Light had begun to take the place of shame and darkness.

The benefits of Telling It are many. First, taking responsibility for your actions and sharing that with God and another person will cause you to live and not die. Confessing is good for the soul and helps us to stop carrying our old, excess baggage. You can get feedback and insight from another caring person, and you can begin to see that you are not alone. Someone may say to you, "I know how you feel," or "I did the same or worse," or "I understand how you could have done that." You may find you have been too hard on yourself.

Telling It can give us peace because we stop running from ourselves and face our past before God and another person. When we let light fall on our hidden darkness, our secrets disappear along with the shame that imprisoned us. This step promises the beginnings of a spiritual experience, of becoming aware of God's presence, of having our fears fall away, and of starting to love and accept ourselves for who we really are.

When you decide who you will share your inventory with, don't procrastinate. Let go of your self-consciousness and pride and go do it.

This can be a time-consuming step. When speaking aloud on the following inventories, here are some suggestions:

The Resentment Inventory Form: Just share columns 1 and 4. It is not necessary to repeat out loud column 2, which is really another person's inventory. Tell what *you* did and what *you* could have done differently.

The Fear Inventory Form: Read what your fears are, why you have them, God's promises for you, and what would God have you be.

Healing from Codependency

Becoming whole and not codependent—getting freed from people pleasing—is not easy and takes practice. The key is: Stop looking to another person for validation of your worth or to make you feel okay about yourself. Don't get absorbed and obsessed in another dysfunctional man's life, which can only keep you distracted from developing yourself and your own life. *Trying to change someone else is an escape from the task of changing yourself, which is the only person you really can change.*

Some of us got so out of touch with ourselves and with God that we became blinded to what we needed to look at in ourselves— namely, the fact that we contributed to our abusive and painful situations. Because we couldn't see our truth, we stayed stunted in our spiritual growth, unable to identify the changes we could make in ourselves to heal and move forward.

The following is a letter-writing exercise that can help you find the connection between how you have been treated by a mate and your part in it. It can also show you where you have a blind spot in the relationship you have with yourself and God.

Begin by writing a letter to the man or the ex- in your life with whom you have had issues. Express what he did or didn't do that hurt and angered at you. This is only an exercise! Do not send this letter to anyone. Just write what you wish the other person had done or been to you:

Dear _____ *,*

　　Sometimes, I wondered how you could hurt me by _____

_____.

　　I just wish you had _____ *, and I wish you*

could have _____.

From,

_____

(Your name)

Now, go back and cross off the other person's name and fill in your *own* so that this letter becomes addressed to *you.* Cross off your signature at the bottom and sign it, "Love, God." Now reread the letter. It will help you find out what God is trying to tell you about yourself through your relationships. Most of us are in the habit of blaming other people for our problems. *Whenever you get the impulse to blame someone else, it's usually you who needs to hear your complaint.* Now go back and reread your letter again.

　　This is hard and painful work, but the payoff is that you can get unstuck and have real change and healing come forth!

Setting Boundaries

Many of us discovered, in our Chapter Four Inventories, that we had allowed unacceptable behavior in our lives from others and that we had been truly unprotected. In order to feel safe and to ward off hurtful behaviors from others, it's important to learn the specifics about boundaries, what they are, and how to set them. Normally, that's something we begin learning as toddlers. But if you didn't learn this in childhood, you need to learn it in adulthood. In abusive or neglectful homes, appropriate boundaries are regularly violated, and we conclude that we are not worthy of reasonable boundaries. But it's never too late to begin establishing appropriate and protective boundaries around your life. Do it now!

Setting boundaries is *your* job in every relationship. It is your work to make clear what treatment is and is not acceptable to you, and likewise you are to declare what you are and are not willing to do for the other person. **Good boundary setting requires understanding the difference between helping someone and enabling them**. When we do something for someone that s/he is not capable of doing for her/himself, that is **helping**, and it is a healthy thing to do. But when we do something that another could and should do for her/himself, that is **enabling**, and that is unhealthy and is symptomatic of codependency.

It is important, when setting boundaries, that you communicate what the consequences will be if the other person crosses those boundaries—and then you must be ready to enforce that. Consistent consequences are essential to others' learning to respect our boundaries. Remember to use the *Serenity Prayer* (*) so that guilt and fear don't prevent you from taking a healthy stand for yourself.

Setting boundaries allows us the freedom to be ourselves. We each have an invisible space around us made up of who we are, what we do, and how we think. Boundaries protect that separateness, and healthy relationships support the other person's uniqueness. That respectful treatment of the other's space is what allows healthy relationships, self-esteem, and self-worth to flourish. When you acknowledge other people's boundaries, you are saying, "I respect you. I free you to be you."

The following are guidelines for setting healthy boundaries. Follow them and write out the boundaries you want to set in your relationships with others:

1. Set limits for what you are willing to do in a relationship.
2. Be specific in your request of others.
3. Be reasonable.
4. Create boundaries that are enforceable.
5. Have boundaries that are natural and logical.

Boundaries have two parts: There is the boundary itself and then there are the consequences for violating that boundary. Write down clear, precise consequences for violating the boundaries you establish. Fill in the blanks in the following sentences to map out a boundary and its corresponding consequence:

"I will not tolerate _____ *(state the unacceptable*

behavior). I will confront that behavior with you and if you

continue that behavior, I will take care of myself by _____
_____ *(state action to be taken)."*

Many of us have low self-esteem because we were fed lies about who we really are. By believing the lies about our identity, we think God must not care about us either. It's important to learn to look at ourselves differently by seeing ourselves through God's eyes. Meditate on the following to know how your Heavenly Father feels about you, especially if you missed the closeness and the love of an earthly father:

Father's Love Letter
An Intimate Message From God To You.
My child . . .
You may not know me but I know everything about you . . . Psalm 132:1
I know when you sit down and when you rise up . . . Psalm 132:2
I am familiar with all your ways . . . Psalm 39:3
For you were made in my image . . . Genesis1:27
In me, you live, you move and have your being . . . Acts 17:28
For you are my offspring . . . Acts 17:28

You were not a mistake . . . Psalm 139:15-16

For all your days are written in my book . . . Psalm 139:15-16

You are fearfully and wonderfully made . . . Psalm 139:14

I knit you together in your mother's womb . . . Psalm 139:13

And brought you forth on the day you were born . . . Psalm 71:5

I am not distant and angry but am the composite expression of love . . . 1 John 3:1

I offer you more than your earthly father ever could . . . Matthew 7:11

For I am the perfect father . . . Matthew 5:48

Every good gift that you receive comes from my hand . . . James 1:17

For I am your provider and I meet all your needs . . . Matthew 6:31-33

My plan for your future has always been filled with hope . . . Jeremiah 29:11

Because I love you with an everlasting love . . . Jeremiah 31:3

My thoughts toward you are as countless as the sand on the seashore . . .
Psalm 139:17-18

And I rejoice over you with singing . . . Zephaniah 3:17

I will never stop doing good for you . . . Jeremiah 32:40

For you are my treasured possession . . . Exodus 19:5

And I want to show you great marvelous things . . . Jeremiah 33:3

If you seek me with all your heart, you will find me . . . Deuteronomy 4:29

Delight in me and I will give you the desires of your heart . . . Psalm 37:4

For it is I who give you those desires . . .Philippians 2:13

For I am your greatest encourager . . . 2 Thessalonians 15-17

I am also the father who comforts you in all your troubles . . . 2 Corinthians 1:3-4

When you are broken-hearted, I am close to you . . . Psalm 34:16

As a shepherd carries a lamb, I have carried you close to my heart. Isaiah 49:11

One day I will wipe away every tear from your eyes . . . Revelation 21:3-4

And I will take away all the pain you have suffered on this earth . . .
Revelation 21:4

I am your father and I love you, even as I love my son, Jesus . . . John 17:23

For in Jesus, my love for you is revealed . . . John 17:28

He is the exact representation of my being . . . Hebrews 1:3

And he came to demonstrate that I am for you, not against you . . . Romans 8:31

And to tell you that I am not counting your sins . . .2 Corinthians 5:18-19

Jesus died so that you and I could be reconciled . . . 2 Corinthians 5:18-19

His death was the ultimate expression of my love for you . . . 1 John 4:10

I gave up everything I love that I might gain your love . . . Romans 8:32

If you receive the gift of my son, Jesus, you receive me . . . 1 John 2:23

And nothing will ever separate you from my love again . . . Romans 8:36-39

Come home and I will throw the biggest party heaven has ever seen . . . Luke 19:7

I have always been father and I will always be father . . . Ephesians 3:14-15

My question is, "Will you be my child?" . . . John 1:12-13

I am waiting for you . . . Luke 15:11-32

Love, your Dad!

Almighty God

Consider adopting a new set of expectations and behaviors that you want to incorporate into the next part of your life. Below are some affirmations to build on. Add others to the list as you think of them. Let your list give you a new standard by which to assess how you are doing in establishing healthy boundaries in relationships:

- I accept responsibility for what I do with my life.

- I love and approve of myself.

- I no longer seek love and approval from a man or any source outside myself.

- I make decisions that protect me and move me away from unhealthy relationships.

- I let go of taking responsibility for other peoples' feelings.

- I support and nurture myself, especially when I feel low.

- When I revert back to unloving behavior, I stop it and recommit to loving and supporting who I am.

Now that you have looked at some of your weaknesses and unhealthy behaviors, you can continue to look at ways to change and develop new, healthier behaviors. Many of us got stuck in toxic relationships and hurtful situations because we believed we were helpless victims without a choice. When you feel really stuck in your life, learn how to focus on solutions rather than problems. It's important to look at what you are asking for. *Ask and you shall receive* is a spiritual principle active in our lives. The questions we ask determine where we focus our attention. So instead of asking, *Why? Ask, What can I do about this situation?* Change a challenge into an opportunity.

When we change our question from "What is wrong?" to "What is the solution?" we change our whole emotional state. So practice looking for the opportunities in your life rather than giving in to victim-paralysis.

Below is a list of questions that perpetuate negative thought patterns and experiences. Below each question is an alternative question that can generate hope, uplift you, and can change the flow of your mind from being problem-oriented to being solution-seeking. These are only a few examples. Use them to help you think of other negative questions you realize you dwell on, and replace them with the others that point toward solutions.

Instead of: "Why?"

Ask: "What can I do?"

Instead of: "Why am I so _____ *(for ex. fat, stupid, etc.)*?"

Ask: "How can I become _____ *(for ex. thinner, wiser)*"

Instead of: "Why don't I have _____ ?"

Ask: "What are some good ways to create _____ ?"

Instead of: "Why am I not succeeding?"

Ask: "What can I do to accomplish _____*(name the outcome)*?"

Instead of: "Why does this always happen to me?"

Ask: "What can I learn from this?"

Questions to Answer:

- What is your resistance to sharing hidden parts of yourself with another person?

- What can be gained by admitting your faults to another person?

- Which of your faults is the most difficult to acknowledge? Why?

- In what ways will admitting to God, to yourself, and to another person prevent you from deceiving yourself?

Scriptures Related to Chapter Five:

James 5:16a   Psalms 32:3-5   Romans 10:10
Romans 3:22-24   Proverbs 28:13   1 John 1:9

Prayer for Chapter Five:

Dear God,

Thank You for letting me speak openly with You and another person about my life. If I have left out anything important, please show me. Help me focus on myself and my relationship with You. Help me heal and take responsibility for my actions as I continue to look at the thoughts, feelings, and choices I have made that have blocked me from Your love. Amen.

SIX

Preparation

Prepare: Get ready for God to take away your character defects. Decide you want to change and believe that God can and will accomplish this change in you. *(James 4:10)*

As our ineffective behaviors become more pronounced and uncomfortable to live with, we become ready to let go and have them removed. In this chapter, we become ready to let *God* remove our character defects. Fortunately, we don't have to do the removing at all; we just have to be ready—willing—for our defects *to be removed*.

Fear, self-seeking, dishonesty, and selfishness are the key shortcomings we need to let God remove from us. Feeling unworthy, seeing ourselves as victims, and our tendency to people-please are other behaviors we can prepare to let God heal and change in us. Our work in Chapters One through Five helped us to get ready for this next important step forward.

The first time I did this work, I did not even realize I was doing it. At the time, I was a love addict and a needy woman, and one of my defects of character was self-centered fear. I was so focused on what I didn't have, and what I wanted to fill the emptiness I felt inside, that I compulsively went from the end of one relationship to the beginning of another.

I did not know how to sit still in the pain I felt and walk through it. I only knew how to react to my feelings, without much or any forethought. When I was single and alone and felt attracted to some-one, I acted on it. The problem was, I continuously got involved with unhealthy or abusive men. My partner-picker was obviously broken, and even though I learned that if I was attracted to a man, he was almost guaranteed to be the wrong one—I went headlong into that next relationship anyway.

Once I finally and truly committed to working on my recovery, I pledged to not date or have a relationship for a year. The first five months went by faster and more easily than I'd expected. But then a new guy showed up at a recovery meeting I went to regularly, and I was immediately attracted to him. He was tall, dark, handsome, and well-dressed, obviously a professional in the community. Our eyes met, and he walked over to me. We introduced ourselves, and he said he was new to the area. He was an ophthalmologist, who was looking to start a new practice here. I began flirting with him, and when he responded with interest, I began questioning my agreement to abstain from men and relationships. My heart raced as I fought the draw to him.

Suddenly, I realized I was acting exactly the way I had always acted around men. Part of me felt the excitement and high of meeting someone new, while another part asked, "What are you doing? You're a lovesick relationship-addict. Don't act impul-sively on feelings of attraction. Remember your commitment: It's you and God right now, and it's time to find yourself first. Keep God in charge."

The eye doctor kept talking, but his words faded into the back-ground noise of the gathering. I couldn't focus on our conversation because the one taking place in my head was too loud.

I excused myself and left the room. I wanted to regroup. I felt like I did when I first gave up drinking or smoking. Before recov-ery, I used to rationalize my addictive urges by telling myself, *If I feel this strongly about doing something, I must need to do it.* Being in recovery had taught me to clean up my life by *not* acting on my feelings as I had impulsively done for a lifetime. I was learning that, just because it felt right, that didn't mean it *was* right.

In the past, I would have been driven to get to know this man. I would have flirted and acted coy. But now I was in a different mode. I sensed God's subtle guidance; it came into my thoughts in words I knew weren't my own and told me, *"Don't act on your attraction to him. Don't participate in your feelings; just wait and watch. Observe him over time and see what happens. Keep your distance and let this new man show you his truth. The truth will give you knowledge about yourself that can change the course of your life forever.*

It was a powerful message, and I followed that inner directive over the next month. I regularly attended the same meetings the new man did, but I didn't converse with him or flirt; I just watched him from a distance. I continued to feel a strong attraction to him, though, and of course I often wondered, *Am I missing the opportunity to meet "the one"?* But even though I was lonely and longing for the fun and excitement of getting to know someone new, I stayed true to my commitment. I just waited and watched.

The good news is, God can remove the stumbling blocks that keep us from attaining our full potential in life. We can't, but He can if we let Him. Those stumbling blocks are our defects of character. Our part in this process is to become willing to let go of old, unhealthy behavior patterns.

How do we become willing? Our stumbling blocks (character defects) become so apparent and troublesome to us that we become ready. I became ready when I decided to listen to God's directives instead of my usual impulses. For the first time, I was ready to have God change me.

Two months later, the eye doctor relapsed on alcohol and drugs. The night before his relapse, he slept with a woman from the meetings whom he had pursued with determination. He had a one-night stand with her, relapsed, then bailed out on her by leaving town. She became pregnant from that one night of poor judgment and was left to raise her baby alone.

I was struck with the thought that that could have been me. I felt compassion for the woman, as though she had taken the consequences that could have been mine, left to my old devices.

The truth stared me down: I was still attracted to the same kind of man who offered the same potential hazards as in my past. I was attracted to men on the basis of lust, not love. I was grateful that I had been saved from another go-around of disappointment, disillusionment, heartache, and single parenting.

I resolved to let any future attractions just wash over me like a nice summer breeze and let them go. The experience of seeing disastrous consequences that could have been mine became a defining moment for the future of my love life.

In some ways, the work of Chapter Six can be called repentance. It is a state of "wanting to change." Ask yourself, "Am I ready and willing to stop trying to fix myself and cooperate with God so He can do His job?" The things we want God to take away are often deeply ingrained patterns of ineffective behavior. They will not disappear overnight. We must be patient while God is transforming and shaping us into new people. For God to remove ineffective behaviors, we must let Him be in control, which means we must relinquish self-will. Up until now, we have identified, opened, and begun cleansing our wounds. In this chapter, we prepare to let God do the healing.

As we identify the negative traits and behaviors within us, we need to suspend judgment and fault-finding about ourselves. Remember that, as we seek to become willing to have our character defects removed, they may intensify for a time, and we may feel as if we are under a microscope or magnifying glass. God will be giving us opportunities to practice making new choices regarding old patterns in our life. The changes in us come as we realize that, through our weaknesses, God makes us capable of what we could not do on our own power.

Turning Weaknesses to Assets

Yet, as we learn to follow God's will and receive our healing, those same character defects can turn into positive strengths as we learn how to set boundaries for ourselves, to be honest with ourselves, to be at peace, and to better connect with God. When we did our

Chapter Four inventories, we may have recognized that our part in contributing to unhealthy and hurtful encounters with others resulted from defects of character and behaviors such as unworthiness, people pleasing, being a victim, trying to fix others, fearing abandonment, being impulsive, and isolating. In Chapter Six, we consider looking at these areas within us and lifting them up for God to heal and transform them.

UNWORTHINESS left us nonassertive, fearing failure and rejection, needing to be perfect and having a negative self-image. As we heal from low self-esteem, we become more confident, we act more assertively, we trust and validate ourselves instead of looking to others to do so. We love and accept ourselves as we really are, having less fear of mistakes because we recognize that we can learn from them. Feeling safer and having less fear, we find we can achieve things we never dreamed possible with confidence and with God.

PEOPLE-PLEASING caused us to ignore our own needs, feel unworthy, lack self-esteem, and fear criticism and failure. As we heal from people-pleasing, we can attend to our own needs, learn to tell the truth about how we feel, become more authentic and trustworthy. We learn to mean what we say and say what we mean, because we seek our own and God's approval first, and stay true to ourselves and God first.

BEING A VICTIM caused us to feel trapped, hopeless, and without a choice or a way out. It left us taking everything personally; feeling constantly stressed, anxious, and mentally/emotionally exhausted from too much unnecessary thinking and feeling. But now we are learning that we are not in control of other peoples' lives, their choices or behaviors, their outcomes and responses. Instead, we focus on ourselves. As we heal, we also learn to take responsibility for our thoughts, feelings, and actions. We discover we have a choice in how we think, and therefore feel, and therefore act. We seek to take captive the thoughts of doubt, fear, and self-pity, and to focus instead on God's promises of hope, faithfulness, provision, and protection. Our intimacy levels increase and our stress levels decrease.

FIXING OTHERS by rescuing, taking care of and advising people, caused us to ignore our own needs, lose our identity, feel guilty and inadequate. We became codependent with our need to be needed. As we heal our need to fix others, we learn to take care of ourselves, develop our own identity and interests, set limits for helping others, and recognize when we are getting into codependent relationships. We become less and less responsible for everyone else and allow individuals to find their own way. We turn people over to God, allowing Him to work out their lives instead of trying to direct another's life, ourselves. By letting go of fixing others, we find time to develop ourselves and our own interests and lifestyles. Instead of obsessively caring for others, we accept that we cannot control other peoples' lives, and acknowledge that we are responsible only for our own lives.

FEARING ABANDONMENT caused us to feel insecure and guilty, and to avoid standing up for ourselves—which also caused us to act and make choices out of codependency and the fear of being alone. As we heal from fear of abandonment, we learn to see that we are worthy, lovable, and valuable. We seek out healthy relationships with people who love and care for themselves and who show concern for us. As we feel more secure, we consider our own needs in a relationship, and we resolve relationship problems by trusting in God. We become drawn to healthier people. Our self-confidence grows as we realize that God will never abandon us, which means we will never again be totally alone.

BEING IMPULSIVE left us at the whim of our emotions, acting rashly on impulsive judgments. As we heal, we learn to trust God and even ourselves, to wait patiently for God's guidance and direction. We feel less stressed, and we enjoy our lives more as we act in obedience and accordance with God's will. We learn that, in time, God's will brings about victory to our challenges; in time, He will use for good anything that was intended for our harm. We find peace as we surrender our will and our lives over to God's care. We use the *Serenity Prayer* whenever we feel compelled to act rashly from anxious fears.

ISOLATING was an unhealthy behavior because we wanted to avoid experiencing fear, being rejected, or being alone. Instead of exposing ourselves to others, we judged ourselves, felt defeated, gave into self-pity, and felt as if we didn't belong. As we heal from isolating, we learn to accept ourselves and others as we are, to express ourselves, to be less self-centered, and to actively participate in life with others. We become more willing to take risks with new people and places; we seek friends and relationships that are more nurturing, safe, and supportive. We get involved in and enjoy group activities. We begin to realize that we belong as much as anyone else.

Chapter Six work is simple. It is really only a moment in time in which we acknowledge our *willingness*. We become willing to enter the process of letting go, and trusting God to help.

The key to becoming ready for change is to identify what we no longer need or want. We can do this because God partners with us, allowing specific people and situations in our day to coincide with the lessons we are learning, giving us opportunities to apply the principles of the step we are currently working on.

Mental Gardening: Taking Thoughts Captive

As we seek to allow God to change our weaknesses into assets, our part in our transformation is to renew our minds. Preparation can help us assess the garden of thoughts that live in our mind. We will take off the rose-colored glasses and identify the weeds growing in our gardens. We want to make room there for the new flowers to grow.

Receiving God's Word offers a renewing of our minds. Our key to change and healing is a biblically transformed mind. God tells us in Romans 12:2, "... *do not be conformed to this world, but be transformed by the renewing of your mind, that you may prove what is that good and acceptable and perfect will of God."* Healing requires us to learn how to think differently, how to change old perceptions, reactions, and the fear of abandonment. God will renew our minds as we continue reading, studying, and applying God's Word to our thinking and lives. We are not our past. When our wounds are healed, that past will no longer trip up our present. God can heal us completely.

Improving our thought-life requires taking captive the thoughts that contribute to a stuck life: doubt, fear, negative thinking, "what if" conversations, depressing self-talk, waiting for the other shoe to drop, self-pity parties, and our tendency to dwell on possible future gloom. These are all weeds growing in our minds and thought-life, and need to be pulled. We have to change how we talk to ourselves, to the world, and to God about our lives. We have to monitor closely our thought-life all the time. Mental gardening means consistently discovering and rooting out the negative, ungodly thoughts right away, instead of giving them time to take root and grow.

Our thoughts are like seeds which grow and affect our emotions. Good seeds, good thoughts, produce joy, peace, love, and happiness. Negative thoughts produce, anger, fear, pain, frustration, and strife. The Bible is like a bag of good seed, filled with God's Word, which is incorruptible and always works to grow good things. Farmers know that leaving seed in the bag, in the barn, won't produce anything, but that seed planted in suitable ground will grow.

Proverbs 4:20-23 says, "*My son, give attention to my words; incline your ear to my sayings. Do not let them depart from your eyes; Keep them in the midst of your heart; For they are life to those who find them, and health to all their flesh. Keep your heart with all diligence, for out of it spring the issues of life.*"

Answer the following questions:

• What weeds growing in your mind need to be pulled out?

• Are there problems in your life that you consider hopeless?

• Are there dreams in your life that you've waited years to see fulfilled?

• Are there dead things in your life that need to come alive?

Jesus used words to raise the dead back to life. When Lazarus lay dead in the tomb Jesus said, "*Lazarus, come forth!*" and He brought him to life. And when Jesus said to the paralyzed man, "*Get up, take your mat and go home,*" the man was healed. And there was the Centurion who had such faith that he told Jesus, "*Just say the word and my servant will be healed.*" Jesus spoke, and the servant was healed from a great distance. In order for things to happen on earth, we must speak it out first. Since we are made in His image, we can speak things into existence, too. You must say it, stand on it, and believe it until it drops out of the unseen spiritual realm into the seen physical realm.

We are constantly speaking out things that we really don't want to have happen, creating self-fulfilling prophecies. Consider how often you make negative statements like, "*I am never going to be able to . . .*" We must be careful not to verbally address the, "*What if's . . .*" of life, or make statements like, "*Things have always been like that . . .*" An overweight person might say, "*Oh, I'm so fat, I'll never get this weight off.*" Or a person with a lot of relationship issues might say, "*I'll never have a good relationship. I don't think I'm capable of it.*"

Sometimes people verbally beat up on themselves with questions that are really statements: "*Why was I so stupid?*" "*What's wrong with me?*" "*Will I ever learn anything?*" That's just another example of how a negative statement can turn into a self-fulfilling prophecy. Pay attention to how you talk to yourself. Proverbs 23:7 tells us, "*For as he thinks in his heart, so is he . . .*"

- List below some negative statements and questions you make about yourself:

The key to seeing bad circumstances give way to good ones is to confess His Word over your situation with a heart of expectation and faith. Proclaim God's Word over your life, regardless of what you are experiencing. The team of your mouth and the Word of God is the greatest weapon you have against temptation, doubt, and evil. Learn how to talk back to the negativity in your life. Don't let it bring you down and control and determine your experience. Speak out loud, saying that you believe God is working in your life and your challenges and in your relationships. That's how you take thoughts captive.

This is exactly what Jesus did when He was tempted by Satan immediately after His forty-day fast in the desert. Satan tried to tempt and entice Jesus, as recorded in Matthew 4:2-4: *And when He had fasted forty days and forty nights, afterward He was hungry. Now when the tempter came to Him, he said, "If You are the Son of God, command that these stones become bread." But He answered and said, "It is written, 'Man shall not live by bread alone, but by every word that proceeds from the mouth of God.'"*

Practice personalizing and speaking God's promises over your life. You can begin by referring to **God's Promises to Well Woman** as listed in the back of this book in the Appendices.

Feeling down is a common byproduct of having weedy thoughts of fear and resentment rooted in our minds. Sometimes negative thoughts are so habitual and repetitive, we're truly unconscious of them. This is why, when we're down, we need to stop and purposefully retrace our thinking. When we find the negative thoughts, we can change them and therefore the subsequent emotions they produced. *We can change how we feel by changing what we think.*

When we lose our peace and serenity, some form of self-will is usually involved. We may either be *afraid of losing what we have* or afraid *of not getting what we want.* When we can identify this, we can let go of our wants and fears and give the outcome to God. Disciplining our mind and emotions, monitoring our thoughts and taking the unhealthy, negative ones captive, is a practice that may need to be done over and over throughout a day to nurture our internal peace. Here's the story of an old Cherokee Indian who understood how to win the battle in your mind:

One evening and old Cherokee told his grandson about a battle that goes on inside people. He said, "My son, the battle is between two wolves, inside us all. One is evil. It is anger, envy, jealousy, sorrow, regret, greed, arrogance, self pity, guilt, resentment, inferiority, lies, false god, false pride, superiority and ego. The other is good. It is joy, peace, love, hope, serenity, humility, kindness, benevolence, empathy, generosity, truth, compassion and faith."

The grandson thought about it for a minute and then asked his grandfather, "Which wolf wins the battle?"

The old Cherokee simply replied, "The one you feed."

To become more of what we want to be and less of what we were, we must practice not letting our minds run wild or focusing on our own will. When we are feeding the ungodly in us, insanity ensues. Happiness doesn't depend on what we have or what we do. It's determined by what we think. So learn to think on good things. God tells us in Galatians 6:7-9: *"Do not be deceived, God is not mocked; for whatever a man sows, that he will also reap. For he who sows to his flesh will of the flesh reap corruption, but he who sows to the Spirit will of the Spirit reap everlasting life. And let us not grow weary while doing good, for in due season we shall reap if we do not lose heart."*

Stop reacting in the same old ways to the same old irritants in your life. God's advice to us is the same as the Cherokee Indian's: Kill the flesh and feed the spirit inside you. Most emotions are responses to our perceptions, which are what we *think* is true about a given situation. If our perception is false, then our emotional response will be based on a false premise and be inappropriate, too. So learn to check on the perceptions that ultimately determine your fears and resentments. The fact that we believe something firmly does not make it true. Be willing to look at what you believe and to keep an open mind to finding truth.

The more you live in the truth, the more your emotions will help you see clearly. John 8:31-32 reminds us, *"Then Jesus said to those Jews who believed Him, 'If you abide in My word, you are My disciples indeed. And you shall know the truth, and the truth shall make you free.'"*

Accomplished athletes or bodybuilders show us what human beings can achieve through consistent disciplined effort. They develop those abilities through rigorous training. Paul wrote in 1

Timothy 4:8, *"For bodily exercise profits a little, but godliness is profitable for all things, having promise of the life that now is and of that which is to come."* Our spiritual muscles and strength, too, develop only as a result of daily effort and discipline. Taking a personal inventory requires such discipline and motivation, but as we look forward to the rewards promised us in this life and beyond, we find the willingness to do the hard work.

It's not a sin to have a bad thought. Bad thoughts do come through our minds. It is a sin if we allow them to remain and we act on them. We must decide to take action to prevent negative thoughts or feelings from building nests in our heads. We need to police our thoughts and our perceptions. We need to learn to say, "I don't believe that, based on what I know from God's Word."

All thoughts are building blocks. If we embrace the first thought that comes to us, before we know it, we'll have another related thought, and another and another. For example, if you embrace the thought, "I'm not that attractive," and dwell on that, your next thought might be, "People don't like me." You'll dwell on that, and then the next thought becomes, "I'm not leaving the house." Before you know it, a fortress of negative thoughts has built up lies in your mind, lies you've allowed to become a stronghold, thought by thought.

Our thought life is a battle and it requires us to spend time and discipline in learning the Word of God. We need to learn which thoughts are aligned with the Word of God and which are not. We must take captive those thoughts that are ungodly, unloving, fearful, and self-defeating. By monitoring and taking captive negative thoughts early on, we can prevent dwelling on them and allowing negative strongholds to be built in our thinking.

Formula for Creating Loving Relationships

As we prepare and become willing to have God remove our defects of character, we learn to turn our focus toward developing ourselves and loving relationships. There are two parts to creating a loving relationship.

Part One: in the space below, list the character traits you desire your relationship partner to have. (I've included some possible examples for you to consider for your list.)

1. _____   Loving and giving

2. _____   Trustworthy

3. _____   Stable — takes care of himself

4. _____   Confident

5. _____   Fun-loving, happy, like a kid

6. _____   Forgiving — makes amends

7. _____   Disciplined

8. _____   Shows self-control

9. _____   Prays and meditates

10. _____   Honest

Part Two: Commit to becoming everything you have written down on the list of what you deserve in a mate. Every day, develop in yourself what you put on your list of qualities you would like to find in a good mate. Complete within yourself what you desire to find in another. This requires a lot of real work!

We must strive to be what God wants us to be. God has given us ten essentials for godly living in Titus 2:3-5: He wants us to become dignified, good, kind, loving, self-controlled, calm, discreet, prudent, and not malicious or gossipers.

Ask yourself this key question: "Have I spent more time looking for the right person or seeking to *be* the right person?"

It's the nature of being human to wish for a loving relationship. But if you want love, you must become loving. What we become will be reflected back to us in our relationships.

If one of the traits you want in someone else is trustworthiness, the best insurance for finding that in another is to become trustworthy yourself. You practice trustworthiness by keeping your word and doing the next right thing. When you make a promise, fulfill it. When your word is good, you can be counted on, and that is vital in a good relationship.

Instead of trying to change the man in your life, become willing to work on changing yourself. Become more loving to yourself. (And that means if you are with someone who is abusing you, practice self-care by removing yourself from harm's way.) Learn to love and accept yourself. As you form a closer, more intimate and real relationship with yourself *and God*, you position yourself to be able to have other relationships that are more whole.

Another exercise to help you become ready to change is to write a list of your shortcomings, the things about yourself that you are willing to change. Open your mind and heart to believe God can change these things in you. List traits you feel contributed to your failed relationships. Consider this your *Fix Me List*.

Here's an example of a *Fix Me List*:

1. Beating myself up constantly. Quickly judging and criticizing myself.

2. Feeling overly responsible for others. Thinking I am at fault for others' shortcomings and poor choices.

3. Having low self-esteem. Feeling inadequate, worthless, or not important enough.

4. Isolating. Being a loner, and feeling uneasy around other people.

5. Lacking communication skills. Having trouble speaking and expressing myself honestly.

6. People-pleasing and approval-seeking.

7. Being offended easily. Being intimidated by angry people.

8. Being a perfectionist. Panicking when I've made a mistake or have a problem.

9. Being codependent. Focusing and living for someone else and habitually choosing relationships with emotionally unavailable people with addictive personalities.

10. Being controlling. Trying to manipulate outcomes of unpredictable events.

11. Being emotionally immature. Getting angry when things don't go my way, and feeling anxious and fearful when things seem out of my control.

12. Denying, minimizing, or stuffing my feelings. Being afraid of my feelings. Overreacting to certain situations, or blowing up from holding things in. Using behaviors like overeating to distract myself from my feelings.

13. Being a victim. Feeling guilty when I stand up for myself or act assertively.

14. Having insecurities. Automatically thinking people are mad at me or don't like me, especially if they disagree with me.

15. Feeling distrustful. Having to fight off thoughts that someone is betraying me when they haven't actually done anything.

16. Being impulsive. Settling for less than what I really want because I jump too soon at the first opportunity.

Many things on our fix-it lists are survival tactics from our youth. Excessive worrying, caretaking, feeling rejected, controlling people, living in denial, manipulating others, being a perfectionist, being a victim, being codependent, isolating—all those tactics served you *then*, but they aren't getting you anywhere *now*. They are lifelong but ineffective attempts to avoid continued abandonment. With that in mind, fill in the *Fix-It List* below, identifying character defects you're ready to have God remove:

1. _____

2. _____

3. _____

4. _____

5. _____

6. _____

7. _____

8. _____

9. _____

10. _____

Now, are you willing to look at some descriptions of a godly woman? In the Bible, the book of Proverbs is filled with practical wisdom for living. In *A Wife of Noble Character* (Proverbs 31:10-31), we find a wonderful description of a godly woman. This Proverb describes what kind of woman we can strive to be, and what kind of woman a man would be wise to marry. She's described as outwardly beautiful, as well as inwardly wise. A godly woman is priceless, and there is no greater gift a good man can be given in his life than her love.

I have listed below some qualities I think describe a godly woman. Read them over and add any you would like. Then check off the ones you would like to partner with God and develop in yourself:

☐ Loves and listens to God

☐ Puts God first in her life

☐ Is trustworthy

☐ Is a loving person

☐ Reaches out to others

☐ Takes good care of herself

☐ Keeps a good balance between relationships and responsibilities

☐ Is generous, thoughtful, and wise

☐ Is hardworking

☐ Has peace and serenity

☐ Is faithful and honest

☐ Stands by through hardship

☐ Is loyal and committed

☐ Seeks self-correction rather than nagging and blaming

☐ Trusts God

☐ Has self-confidence and is encouraging to others

☐ Appreciates and honors her mate

☐ Seeks to support his needs

☐

☐

☐

☐

Questions to Answer:

- What do you fear about having your character defects removed?

- Identify two character defects you are not ready to have removed:

- Do you believe God can remove your shortcomings?

- What does each of those defects do "to" you and "for" you?

- How has each of the old tools for coping with your life out-lived its usefulness?

- What harm is it doing to you to cling to each of these old ways of thinking and acting?

Scriptures Related to Chapter Six:

James 4:10   Psalms 37:4-6   James 1:5-6
1 Peter 1:13   Philippians 3:13-14   Romans 5:20

Prayer for Chapter Six:

Dear God,

*Help me to be willing to let go of what I do not need. Create in me
a clean heart, O God, and renew a steadfast spirit within me. Amen.*

SEVEN

Asking God's Help

Ask God: Ask God to help you change. Let God heal you, forgive you and love you. Accept the changes that He makes in you. (*1 John 1:9*)

It's simple. Don't delay. To ask God means to pray humbly. To be humble means to set aside our prideful, selfish behaviors and surrender our will to God's guidance so that we may receive the peace and happiness we seek.

The action required here is *asking*. We ask a Power greater than ourselves to remove from us all that blocks us from living useful lives. It's important to do what we *can* do toward healing, growth, and change, and to trust God to do what we can't. We express humility by not worrying and by not saying, "Excuse me, God, I think I can take care of this on my own."

Having been raised by atheist parents, and having experienced mental, emotional, and sexual abuse throughout a stressful and challenging childhood, my search for God began when I was twenty-four years old. That's when I was diagnosed with cancer. After leaving the doctor's office with the frightening news, I said, "God, if you exist, I want to know who You are." But having had no exposure to the power of God through his Word, I began searching for answers in all the wrong places, always trying to fix myself with self-help. I went from one empty well to another, from one phony promise of healing and deliverance to the next. I read up on near-death experiences, on Nostradamus, Hopi prophecy, and the Mayan prophecy calendar. I traveled extensively, during this period, looking for vortexes, sun dials, and pyramids. I read every new self-help book that hit the bookstores.

I was so desperate that I was willing to do anything, even if it made no sense at all. Once, I read that if you place crystals wrapped with copper wire under your mattress in a certain geometric pattern, it would rework network receptors in your brain and you would be healed from depression. So I flipped my mattress over and connected crystals with copper wire and hoped for emotional relief.

Because of my difficult upbringing, I didn't trust anyone, and I was happier thinking that if I had the right information, I could fix myself. Self-help books offered an endless array of opportunities! The problem, of course, was that one book said that if I would do this, I could heal myself, and another book would come out saying I had to do *that* to heal myself. Then, of course, another new book came out with yet another approach—and then still another new book followed with even other different and conflicting ideas. I ended up reading book after book and spending lots of time and money searching for do-it-yourself fixes.

I was desperate—for exactly what I have today: peace, joy, and freedom from the bondage of self-destructive habits. Over time, however, the more I tried to fix my life myself, the worse it got. None of those efforts had any lasting effect or resulted in significant change in my life. It was a long and fruitless journey. I saw God fix other people, so I knew He could, but until I discovered the work we'll talk about here in Chapter Seven, I thought I had to figure out how to make my transformation happen myself.

When I gave myself over to the work in this chapter, and truly wanted to give up self-destructive habits, I decided to apply the principles in Chapter Seven to my twenty-five-year cigarette habit. Previously, I had tried every known method to quit, but had never succeeded beyond a few months. I'd tried the patch, hypnosis, smoking cessation classes, smokeless plastic cigarettes, using filters designed to taper off nicotine dependency, and smoking brands I didn't like. Nothing worked. I was frustrated and felt hopeless.

Then, one day, I gave the problem to God to fix. I prayed that He would remove the desire from me, that I would be freed from using cigarettes to hurt myself repeatedly every day. But even after I prayed, to my dismay, I still had the desire and I smoked even more.

Every day, I prayed for help with this problem, seemingly with no relief. Then the miracle happened. Three months into my praying, I woke up without the desire to smoke. The compulsion seemed to have just magically and miraculously disappeared through no effort of my own. It felt strange because it just wasn't there. I didn't smoke that day. I thought about a cigarette many times but I was given the ability to not act on that thought and to resist the temptation.

The following day, the same thing happened, and days turned into two weeks, which became a month—and now I have not smoked a cigarette for over thirteen years. An interesting side note is that, a few months after I quit smoking, I met the man who would become my husband, and he happened to mention that he couldn't stand cigarette smoke!

I know that the promise in this chapter works because scientific research has established that nicotine can be as hard to kick as heroin. That was true for me. I am so glad that I am not responsible for changing in myself what only God can do for me. Lifting away my desire to smoke could only have come from a Power greater than myself, for all my human striving had not been able to accomplish it. God's help may not come as fast or in the way we want it, but it will be accurate, and fruitful, and lasting.

Chapter Seven's work is about partnering with God for our healing and wholeness. We cannot take credit for the actual results of this process. But we are responsible for doing the necessary footwork to allow it to happen. In my example of asking God for help in quitting smoking, my "footwork" was the willingness to be relieved of this self-destructive behavior, and my asking God for His help.

Claiming Our True Identity

One way in which we can cooperate with God, as He changes us, is to believe God's promises, declare and stand on them, until they drop out of the spiritual realm into our lives. There is creative power in the act of confessing aloud God's promises, thereby bringing ourselves into agreement with them. Call them into being. God wants us to have our words line up with His will and His heart. God loves us and wants us to know that He cares about every breath we take and every word we speak.

As we confess His promises boldly, God will deliver us, promote us, heal us, bless us, equip us, and help us. God's Words, spoken through us, literally wield power. But it's not a "name it and claim it" game with God. We can't call on His power while living out of our own selfish desires. We must couple speaking God's promises with being obedient to Him. With faith and persistence, we will either see His promise come to pass, or we will be led by God in another direction. Proverbs 18:21 tells us, *"Death and life are in the power of the tongue, and those who love it will eat its fruit."* The power to influence the direction of our lives—toward life or death—is found in what we speak.

We can think of God's Word as God's will for man, so pick something from Scripture that applies to the situation you're in and believe in its promise. Doubt whittles away at our faith, but God's Word, spoken aloud and acted on, produces results. You can begin by reviewing the promises listed in the Appendices in the back of this workbook entitled **God's Promises for Well Woman.**

God promises that we can have joy and rest even in big troubles. God says there is a *purpose* for our troubles, and that purpose is to develop faith and patience. (James 1:2-6, 12) He even calls those who must endure temptation "blessed."

If we focus on the good that will eventually come out of troubled times, it enables us to feel joy and rest in the midst of the challenge. Speaking God's promises for our future feeds our faith, which is where our rest is found.

If we want to live a blessed life, we need to talk to ourselves differently and start declaring God's goodness. Change is an inside job; it must occur within us before we see it on the outside. As discussed in Chapter Six, most of our beliefs and our word choices have been programmed and reinforced over the span of our lives. In order to change, we must become aware of the words we speak and the thoughts we entertain—because they all count. We all have internal dialogues with ourselves.

The more accurately we select words that are in line with God's will, the faster our desires (the ones that are aligned with His will for you) will take form. Below are samples of affirmations and declarations based on God's promises. Read the following aloud:

- I am forgiven.
- I am restored.
- I am anointed.
- I am equipped.
- I am victorious.
- This is my season.
- God has called me.
- I have what it takes.
- I have a bright future.
- God is pleased with me.
- God is a lover and giver.
- Blessings chase me down.
- I am the head, not the tail.
- I am flowing with creativity.
- I am the apple of God's eye.
- I have clear direction in my life.
- I have a positive outlook on life.
- Good things are coming my way.
- I have faith, favor, and fulfillment.
- I am a child of the Most High God.
- I am blessed with God's mystical wisdom.
- Signs, wonders, and miracles will follow me.

- No weapon formed against me shall prosper.
- I am blessed with self-control and self-discipline.
- I have success, promotion, and Divine protection.
- Through my weakness, God reveals His strength.
- It's not how we start that counts, but how we finish.
- I can do all things through Christ, who strengthens me.
- I am surrounded with great friends and a spiritual family.
- God made this day, and I will be glad and celebrate in it.
- God has not given me a spirit of fear, but of love and of sound mind.
- I was created to feel good about myself, not to struggle against myself.
- I declare that any negative words ever spoken over me are broken in this very instant.

Gaining Self-Confidence

When we have low self-esteem, we tend to isolate and keep to ourselves, not participating with others in living life. If we weren't paid attention to as children, over time we may have decided not to bother making ourselves heard. Maybe we started telling ourselves we didn't matter. If we feel invisible, it's easy to retreat more and more into ourselves and not speak up at all. It's easy to lose our voice, our self-expression, and our power. Feeling powerless can leave us feeling defeated, withdrawn, and not wanting to speak.

When we're rejected as children, we are left with a lot of unfinished life business, so we end up reproducing that same pain in our adult relationships and situations. Correcting how we think about ourselves is essential, since our sense of worthiness affects how we allow others to treat us. Real and lasting self-worth is not based on anything outside ourselves. Bank accounts and employment status can change in the twinkling of an eye and cannot determine our value.

Realize that people can't make you feel a certain way. Your feelings come from within *you*, from the way you learned to feel about yourself in childhood. Ask yourself: When are you going to stop letting outside influences dictate the way you feel about yourself?

The truth is, you *are* visible. You *do* matter. You have a God who loves you a lot. John 8:31-32 says, *"Then Jesus said to those Jews who believed Him, 'If you abide in My word, you are My disciples indeed. And you shall know the truth, and the truth shall make you free.'"*

We can feel confident regardless of how others respond to us. We are no longer the wounded little child who needs to disappear. We can't change or control people. God is in charge and everything is happening just as it needs to, whether we can see it or not. God knows what He is doing when He allows people, places, and things into our lives that bring up buried pain and trigger our emotions. Sometimes we encounter these painful situations and people because our infected wounds must be lanced and drained before they can heal.

We all form ideas about ourselves based on what our parents, friends, classmates, siblings, and teachers tell us, beginning when we are very young. As adults, we make it very clear how we now see ourselves, based on those destructive beliefs we absorbed as children, and our co-workers, employers, neighbors, lovers, family, and friends simply reflect back to us who we think we are and how we feel about ourselves. If we grew up in an environment with people who were critical of us, that is what we see in our internal mirror: someone worthy of criticism. Those criticisms are not necessarily true, but we believe them and therefore see them in our mirror. On the other hand, if we are raised in a loving, supportive environment, where people encouraged and complimented appropriately, then that is the person we see in our mirror. What we see is an accurate reflection of what we learned to see as children.

We can change what we believe about ourselves and what we see in the mirror. We do matter, but we have to take the risk to find that out. Even if we were never the apple of our earthly father's eye, God says we are the apple of His. We no longer need to look to men who reinforce our negative self-image. The key is to get right with our Maker and ask Him to change our inaccurate self-perceptions. And why do we need to do this? Because low self-esteem can silence us and keep us from being assertive. We need a voice and visibility to express the truth about our needs, feelings, and boundaries. God will help us break free from our negative self-image.

You can't change or control others, so instead of giving in to their negative messages, or hanging back, isolating, allowing distance to grow between you and others—participate and regain the expression of your voice. Eventually, when we find and fill our own lives with the truth of what God created us to be, what others do and how they react to us won't feel so profoundly painful. Their messages won't be our source of value, affirmation, and confidence.

Not only can we change how we see ourselves, we can change how we treat our selves. It helps to practice acts of love toward ourselves, rather than waiting for someone else to do that for us. Practice the following simple exercise to start changing how you see yourself. Don't let feeling self-conscious stop you from practicing mirror talk. With repeated practice, you can change how you feel about yourself:

Practice mirror talk. Look in the mirror daily and tell yourself, "I love you!" Then tell yourself the following;

"You're getting better every day!"   "You're beautiful!"
"You're terrific!"   "Nice going!"

Focus on Your Attributes. Fill in the blanks and spend time acknowledging your own divine perfection:

a. I do great at _____.

b. I love this about myself _____.

c. I can _____ really well.

d. People love _____ about me.

e. I have nice _____.

We can become confident! The more we rely on God's will, and trust Him, the more our self-confidence grows. As it grows, we see increasing evidence of His miracle-working presence in our lives. Our fear of abandonment diminishes as we realize that we will never be totally alone again. As that fear diminishes, we become more comfortable being alone, and we lose the need to *care-take* and *people-please.* We begin to consider our own needs, which is a function of self-esteem. We feel safer sharing our honest feelings with others because we feel good about who we are and how we feel about things. And when others do validate us, we don't depend on them to continue doing so, and our relationships grow healthier. We come to understand that we are everything we need to be because we are God's own children. (2 Corinthians 3:5)

Many of us feel a surge of self-confidence when we begin a relationship. We think it is the arrival of a new man that boosts our self-esteem. In reality, it has more to do with giving ourselves permission to look at ourselves through a different lens. When falling in love, we think our new self-confidence has its source in our new partner. The truth is, if we struggle with low self-esteem, often it is only the *idea* of the new partner, and how we think he/she feels about us, that gives us our new high self-esteem. The real key is that we have given our self permission to feel good about ourselves!

Have you ever wondered why, when a relationship ends, your self-confidence disappears, too? It's because *you stopped giving yourself permission to feel good about yourself.* It's never the other person who generates the confidence in us, even if it feels that way. No one else can give us *self*-confidence. Confidence comes from the way we think about ourselves.

We need to acknowledge who God says we are and regard ourselves with love, so that we can develop a different view of ourselves. God is love, and He is in us, so we can feel His love within any time we choose. Start looking at yourself through God's eyes, start accepting and loving yourself right now. Don't wait until some future moment. Don't say, "I'll love myself when . . ." *When* may never come. Practice accepting who you are, as you are, in this moment.

We have a Heavenly Father who is powerful, loving, and forgiving toward us. Maybe your poor sense of self could be solved by asking His help to change your thinking and behaviors. Practice seeing yourself differently; practice developing a truer sense of identity based on how God sees you. The following is a list of truths rooted in Scripture that you can speak out loud. Let yourself feel a new sense of pride as you confess your true identity:

I WAS CREATED IN GOD'S IMAGE. (Genesis 1:27)

I AM LOVED. (Romans 5:8)

I AM CHOSEN BY GOD. (John 15:16)

I AM A NEW CREATION. (2 Corinthians 5:17)

I'M AN HEIR OF GOD THROUGH CHRIST. (Galatians 4:7)

I HAVE THE FRUIT OF GOD'S SPIRIT IN ME OF LOVE, JOY, PEACE, LONGSUFFERING, KINDNESS, GOODNESS, FAITHFULNESS, GENTLENESS, SELF-CONTROL. (Galatians 5:22-23)

I AM FORGIVEN OF SIN. (1 John 1:9)

I AM GIVEN GOD'S PEACE. (John 14:27)

I AM GOD'S OWN CHILD. (Ephesians 1:5)

I AM A CHILD OF THE LIGHT. (Ephesians 5:8)

I AM A CITIZEN OF HEAVEN. (Philippians 3:20)

I AM PART OF A ROYAL PRIESTHOOD. (1 Peter 2:9)

I CAN GIVE MY WORRIES TO GOD. (1 Peter 5:7)

GOD IS FOR ME AND HE IS ON MY SIDE. (Romans 8:31)

GOD IS WORKING OUT EVERYTHING IN MY LIFE FOR
   GOOD. (Romans 8:28)

I AM GOD'S CREATIVE HANDY WORK. (Psalm 139:13-14)

GOD HAS PREPARED GOOD THINGS FOR ME TO DO.
   (Ephesians 2:10)

Don't you want to learn to love who you are and be completely comfortable in your own skin? You can have that confidence and dignity. Confidence not only comes from what we think; it comes also, from what we do. Confidence comes from doing the next right thing, which includes being kind to yourself and others.

Before we have a spiritual program of recovery, we often give in to our emotions and do what *feels* right. Doing what *is* right often does not coincide with our own emotional desires. We develop emotional and spiritual maturity by bypassing the temptation to do what *feels good* in the moment, and by doing what *is* right, instead. Doing esteem-able acts is what raises and builds our self-esteem, and taking care of ourselves with love is an esteem-able act.

Practicing Self-Love and Self-Care

While we ask God to do the work of removing defects that block us from a full relationship with Him and others, we must do our part and stop behaving in ways that are hurtful to ourselves and others. Even though we have turned this process over to God, and have asked for His help, we need be aware of our tendency to repeat old behavior patterns. As God changes us, we need to love and re-parent the wounded child within us, which is also in the process of maturing and evolving spiritually, mentally, emotionally, and behaviorally. Doing this work is doing our part in cooperating with God.

Here are suggestions to incorporate into your daily life to generate and demonstrate loving self-care:

Choose Joy. It is the natural elixir of life. You are only a moment away from feeling it. Joy is not determined by outer circumstances. Real joy comes from inside us. It is knowing that we are intimately loved, cared for, and known by God. Joy comes from choosing to live a surrendered life with God.

Take Care of Your Physical Needs. Learn to nurture your body. It is the temple which houses your spirit.

Drink Plenty of Water. Drink at least six to eight glasses a day. It will cleanse your kidneys and aid your body by eliminating toxins. It will keep you from getting dehydrated, and it will help curb your appetite.

Feed Yourself Happy and Wholesome Foods. Foods that are in their most natural state are closest to the way nature intended them to be consumed. They carry the most unadulterated nutrients.

Give Yourself Enough Rest. Get adequate sleep. Don't wait until your body creates an illness to force you to slow down and nurture yourself. Rest when you need it.

Create Time for Exercise and Relaxation. Walking, stretching, and exercising will help keep your body limber and healthy. Spend time relaxing. When was the last time you watched a sunset at the end of the day, or woke up early enough to welcome the sunrise?

Take Pride in Your Appearance. Put on your favorite outfit, fix your hair, and choose to put your best foot forward for yourself. You'll feel better for it.

Beautify Your Surroundings. Our outer world often reflects our inner world. Simplify your life and your surroundings. As you clean and care for your living space, you will feel better inside. Get rid of clutter. Give away things you don't need or use. Greater clarity and peace will result from getting rid of excess baggage.

Receive Compliments. When you reject a compliment, not only are you putting yourself down, but you're invalidating the other person's opinions as well.

Give Yourself Gifts. We all feel good about receiving presents and going out to special places. Rather than hoping someone else will read your mind and give you what you want, do it for yourself. If you were going to give yourself a gift, what would your first choice be? Second choice?

Be Creative. Explore ways to creatively express yourself and your ideas through some form of art, music, or writing.

Write a Daily List of Goals. Each morning, write out a list of things you would like to accomplish that day. This will help you budget your time, and you will become more organized and productive. Keep your list realistic, crossing off the tasks as you complete them. Whatever you don't complete at the end of the day, add to the beginning of the following day's To Do list.

Become Your Own Best Friend. Love and care for who you are. Do for yourself things you would quickly do for others.

Give Yourself a Pat on The Back. Don't beat yourself up when you are down. That's when you need your love the most. Support who you are. Stand up for yourself, even when everything seems to have gone wrong.

Trust Yourself. Trust that God is guiding you and teaching you through all the events and challenges of your life. You're not the same person you were yesterday. Trust in who you are and what you know today. Become your own greatest confidant.

Develop Humility. Be willing to look at each situation and person in your life as a brand-new experience. Let go of past expectations and future assumptions of what might happen. Do not limit potential outcomes by expecting the future to be what you have experienced in the past. God's Kingdom yields different results from the defeats of our past, including victory over those defeats.

Be Yourself. Be honest and say what you need. Don't be afraid to tell others how their behavior affects you. Be willing to create healthy boundaries in your relationships.

Be Hopeful. Focus on the possibilities and potentials in your life. Trust God to lead you to your destiny. Don't quit five minutes before the miracle happens.

Develop an Attitude of Gratitude. Be thankful for the good in your life. The more thankful we become, the more we will have to be thankful for!

Associate with Emotionally Healthy People. Hang with the winners. Connect with people who are kind and supportive of your needs.

Encourage and Support Yourself. Every evening, review the successes you've had that day. Give yourself credit. Focus on the feelings of worth and confidence that come from your victories. Dwell on the wins and allow the losses to roll off your back like water.

Live and Let Live. You are not responsible for other people's choices, experiences, or feelings. You can be there for them and love them, but it is not up to you to live their lives for them. Everyone has free will to choose how they deal with whatever life brings. Don't interfere with other people experiencing the consequences of their behaviors. When you do, you rob them of their dignity and their opportunity to find God themselves.

Be Free to Live Your Own Life. You do not have to fulfill other peoples' expectations of you. You are ultimately responsible for the results of your actions. You have the right to live your life as you choose. If you fail, you can learn from the experience. Failure is only the opportunity to acquire more wisdom on your particular pathway.

Read, Pray, and Meditate on God's Word. With the amount of negative messages and lies we've all been exposed to in the past, we can't over-feed ourselves on God's love and truth. Have quiet time when you can acknowledge God and your inner connection to Him.

Write Your Plans for Your Life and Give God the Eraser!

Philippians 4:13 says, *"I can do all things through Christ who lives in me."* Self-confidence increases as we learn to rely more and more on the will of God. When we transfer our dependence on others to trust in God, as we become God-dependent, our self-confidence grows. As we begin to realize that, with God in our lives, we will never be totally alone again, our fear of abandonment diminishes and is replaced by feelings of worthiness.

As we do the work of Chapter Seven, we begin to realize that we are somehow different. We have changed. The change is often noticed by others before we become aware of it. The approval-seeking person begins to function more appropriately; the control-addict becomes warmer and more relaxed; the super-responsible individual is no longer victimizing himself by doing for others what they can do for themselves.

As our fear of abandonment leaves us, we begin to be more honest about our feelings, and we begin to consider our own needs in a relationship. As our self-esteem rises, we are able to interact with others and accept ourselves better. As we become more comfortable in our own skin, we get to know others and let them know us better, and we feel safer. As we start trusting and validating ourselves, instead of looking to others for that, our relationships become healthier. As our confidence grows, we act more assertively, and are able to openly express our feelings and to take risks. To experience God's miraculous transforming power, all we have to do is ask for it, and then do our part to receive His love while we also love ourselves for who we are.

Questions to Answer:

- How are you benefiting from God's presence in your life?

- What special blessings has God sent to you since you began practicing these steps?

- List examples of how you are decreasing in self-centeredness and surrendering your will to God.

- Which of your negative character traits are becoming positive?

- Explain how this change is impacting your life.

Scriptures Related to Chapter Seven:

1 John 1:9	James 4:6-8, 10	Psalms 51:1-2
Philippians 4:6-7	1 Peter 5:6-7	Acts 3:19

Prayer for Chapter Seven:

Dear God,

I offer You all of me, good and bad, and ask that You remove those character defects that keep me from Your love and from being useful to You so that I may better do Your will and help others. Please give me the strength and courage to continue on this path with You always. Amen.

Making Peace
With Others . . .

Better keep yourself clean and bright; you are the
window through which you must see the world.

—George Bernard Shaw

Steps eight and nine are the part of the solution
where we clean out the house and set our wrongs
right.

EIGHT

Make a List

Make a List: Make a list of whomever you have hurt, and put yourself on the top of that list. Briefly describe whom you hurt and what you did. Don't look at what they did to you; just focus on what you did to them. (*Luke 6:31*)

The work of this chapter is key to growing spiritually, finding freedom, and becoming more useful to God. Making amends is about restitution and forgiveness. This is how we put our lives back in order: We begin the process of healing damaged relationships through our willingness to make amends for past misdeeds.

Preparing to make amends, we write a list of people we have hurt—and most of us need to put the relationship we have had with ourselves at the top of the list. We can then refer back to our Chapter Four Resentment Inventory list and write down the harm we caused others in reaction to the harm they caused us. Then we add to our list any others we have harmed through our past behaviors.

Up front, we do the hard work, and later, as a result, we experience God's promises.

Through this work, we practice letting go of blaming others and taking responsibility for our past. We come out of isolation and move toward healthy relationships. Letting go of the painful memories and circumstances from the past, we open the door to a new life based on living in peace with ourselves and others, one day at a time, in the present. We learn to let go of the past so that we can embrace the future that God has for us. What has happened in the past is past, and what we do about the past will control our future. This process helps us to let go of our resentments and begin to overcome the guilt, shame, and low self-esteem we have carried for so long. We give careful thought to what we did, when, and to whom. By doing so, we can partner with God and change our behavior.

If we have diligently done the work of the first five chapters, we have become aware of the harm we have caused others. We may even see that we have become our own worst enemies by the choices we made or the attitudes we have had toward others. As we make a list of those persons we have harmed, we do so with the intent of one day making face-to-face admissions of our past wrongs and conflicts. But all we are doing in *this* step is making the list.

Until I came into recovery, my habit was to feel like the victim who always got the short end of the stick. I believed what happened to me was everybody else's fault, and I was miserable. So when I had to make a list of whom I had hurt, I put myself on the top of the list. I listed the ways I had hurt myself over the years. The first one was glaringly obvious the moment I wrote it: I had tried to do myself in with drinking, drugging, and eating. I behaved in those ways to make myself sick, to escape what I felt, and to stuff my feelings. I wanted to make myself and my pain disappear.

I listed other ways in which I had hurt myself. I had been mean to myself. I had verbally beaten up on myself when I was sad, hurt, or frightened. I had continually put myself down, criticizing and judging every word I said and every deed I did, mercilessly. In my mind, I was never good enough. I could never do enough to feel okay about who I was. I felt guilty if I did something good for myself and endlessly sorry if I thought I had done something wrong. I had been my own worst enemy. If I had spoken to anyone else the way I spoke to myself, I would have been accused of harassment.

Next, I listed the dangerous situations I had put myself in with men because I wanted to be loved and didn't want to hurt someone's feelings by standing up for myself.

As I looked over my list, I realized my biggest abuser in my adult life had been *me*. I had not been the victim, as I'd always thought. Suddenly, I was seeing myself as a volunteer who had unknowingly and repeatedly placed myself in destructive situations. I had let the abusers of my childhood live on in my head, enjoying rent-free residency there. They had become a committee of voices I was used to hearing, a committee that totally disregarded my needs. The principles in Chapter Eight showed me who had been holding me hostage all along and who was keeping me from the peace and love in my life that I so desperately desired. It was me, myself.

I began to make an amends to myself by retraining the adult in me to speak and respond appropriately to the inner, wounded child in me. I told her repeatedly each day that I loved her and wanted her to live. I practiced speaking words of life over myself and making many lifestyle changes to nurture and affirm myself. I claimed and spoke out loud: *I am important, I am not guilty, I am loved, and I have the right to be my authentic self. I can have needs, identify them, and put a voice to them.* Chapter Eight's work opened the door to making amends to the most important person on my list: my wounded inner child.

When we express our anger toward others by hurting ourselves, and when we engage in self-defeating behaviors, we need to forgive ourselves, as well. Maybe we hurt ourselves by using things like alcohol, drugs, tobacco, sex, gambling, or shopping to make ourselves feel better, or maybe we placed ourselves in harm's way by staying in a dangerous or unhealthy relationship. We may ask, "How can I forgive myself?"

Everyone has these struggles. Romans 3:23-24 says, " . . . *all have sinned and fall short of the glory of God."* We need to seek God's wisdom as to how we can make amends for the wrongs we have done to ourselves. We do so by giving to ourselves what the person who hurt us couldn't and didn't know how to give. Be willing to love and forgive yourself. Make amends to yourself by changing and taking responsibility for your actions. Have reasonable expectations for yourself, and in faith, turn your worries over to God.

Fill in the blanks regarding a past event:

I want to make an amends to myself for _____
(the harm done).

I forgive myself for all the words that I said out of fear, thoughtlessness, anger, or confusion. I forgive myself for anything I may have done through my past thoughts, words, or actions by which I have caused myself harm.

These are the actions I am willing to take to make things right:

_____

_____

The willingness to forgive ourselves, as well as those who have harmed us, is key to our healing. We have already seen, through our work in previous chapters, that harboring resentments can destroy our serenity and well-being. Harboring resentments is more harmful to us than to the people we resent. We can turn to God for help in practicing forgiveness and acceptance, and in letting go of old issues that may never be resolved. When we identify the damage we've done and seek to correct it, we decrease the chances of repeating our unhealthy behavior patterns.

We begin by accepting and forgiving ourselves so that we can accept and forgive others. If we do not forgive others and accept them as they are, we cannot make a sincere amends with an attitude of dignity, self-respect, and humility. We make amends for our own benefit, and making amends without extending forgiveness to others can lead us into further arguments or disputes, which can neither accomplish anything nor contribute to our peace and healing.

This is the time to be honest and to take responsibility for our own actions without excusing or justifying them or comparing our wrongdoings to theirs. The harm we experienced was often the direct result of not taking action to remove ourselves from harm's way, thereby enabling abuse to continue. Sometimes, out of fear of abandonment, we tried to change, control, or manipulate others to get them to act the way we wanted, instead of allowing them to be themselves. We may have created dependency and tried to control other people in an effort to maintain the relationship as we wanted it to be. We may have lashed out at someone when confronting an issue we felt guilty about, instead of looking honestly at ourselves. Sometimes we harmed our relationships by behaving aggressively and or in an intimidating manner towards others out of frustration over our lack of control. Maybe we were indiscriminate with sexual behavior, and kept true intimacy at bay.

Consider some of the following questions as you make your list of ways in which you harmed others, including those who harmed you:

- Did you cause harm by trying to escape your emotions and choices with careless overspending and shopping?

- Did you cause persistent financial problems and difficulties for your family or others?

- Did you harm yourself more than others when you became angry?

- Did you ignore your own needs and give in to long bouts of depression or self-pity?

Sometimes our anger and hurt seem justified. When someone has truly wronged us, it is possible that we only owe amends for the way we reacted to them. **Making amends involves figuring out how a relationship or situation went wrong, determining our part**

in it, and doing what we can to make it right. I am not saying it is your job to find a way to make an abusive relationship right. But you can "right" your part in the problem by owning responsibility for having participated in it. It is important to know that, in a case of a violent relationship, you would not want to put yourself in harm's way, and you are certainly not expected to physically go to your abuser and say "I'm sorry."

Nonetheless, there will probably be people who belong on your amends list even though that doesn't seem fair to you. They belong there because resenting them only perpetuates your suffering and problems. We *must* look at our part in every problem if we truly want to be free of all of them.

If you find yourself feeling justified in your anger towards someone or some situation, answer the following questions:

- Have you adopted some of his/her character defects?

- Can you, too, say hurtful things in a fit of anger?

- Do you beat up on yourself?

- Are you continuing to abuse yourself the way you have allowed others to?

- Are you hurting yourself in other ways and using another person's wrongdoing as a justifiable excuse for doing so?

- Are you continuing to use another's wrong behavior to justify *your* reactions to the abuse?

With an open mind and a humble heart, coupled with a desire to know peace rather than to be right, start by making a list of the people you have harmed and/or feel uncomfortable about. Without concern for the details, just fill out Column 1. The list may include family members, business associates, friends, creditors, neighbors. It is important to be thorough, so don't worry about how long your list is.

When you have completed Column 1, fill out Column 2. Keep in mind the many types of harm for which you may want to make amends: borrowing or spending extravagantly; stinginess; spending in an attempt to buy friendship or love; withholding money in order to gratify yourself; cheating, injuring, or damaging persons or their property; inappropriate behavior; immoral actions; unethical conduct; setting a bad example for children, friends or others who look to you for guidance; being preoccupied with selfish pursuits; using other people; broken promises; verbal abuse; lack of trust; lying; turning from God; neglecting your obligations to yourself, to family, and to community; allowing them to cause harm to yourself; showing no gratitude toward others who have helped you; being inattentive to others.

As you proceed to Column 3, keep in mind that you can make living amends with your new life and behaviors. That change—living differently—is making amends to your loved ones, friends, and family. Seek God's guidance to live a life of patience, tolerance, peace, and love.

We can make person-to-person amends where there is a need for specific compensation for harm we've done. There are also indirect amends for situations in which it is not possible to make direct amends to the person we harmed. In that case, we could make amends by writing a letter and not mailing it, or by sending it anonymously; by making a change in our self, such as learning to say "no" or by no longer being a victim. In some cases, making amends takes the form of speaking up for ourselves and not letting others do us more harm.

Chapter Eight Amends List

Name the Person You've Harmed:	The Harm You've Done to that Person:	What Will You do to Make Amends?	Are you Ready to Make Amends?		
			Now	Sometimes	Never

Forgiveness

A key to practicing forgiveness toward others is to remember the many things for which God has forgiven *you*. God doesn't want us to use other peoples' wrongdoing as an excuse for acting wrongly ourselves, or for losing faith in Him. He wants us to work toward reconciliation with the important people in our lives. Forgiveness heals and we are greatly enriched when we let go of resentments and let go of the past. So when a loved one wrongs us, we are told, in Matthew 18:21-22, to forgive repeatedly: *"Then Peter came up to Him and said, 'Lord, how many times may my brother sin against me and I forgive him and let it go? [As many as] up to seven times?' Jesus answered him, 'I tell you, not up to seven times, but seventy times seven!'"* (AMP)

A quick calculation: 7 X 70 = 490 times. If that seems like a lot to ask, consider this question: How many times do you want God to forgive *you*? Matthew 6:14 tells us, *"For if you forgive other people when they sin against you, your heavenly Father will also forgive you."* Furthermore, when we forgive someone, we are unburdening ourselves of the job of judge, a position that isn't ours to begin with. God is the only one who can deal with that person, because God is the only judge and vindicator.

Forgiveness brings peace. We need to forgive to keep evil from getting an advantage over us. We need to recognize that it isn't really people and personalities we're fighting, but unseen elements operating behind them, as described in Ephesians 6:12: *"For we do not wrestle against flesh and blood, but against principalities, against powers, against the rulers of the darkness of this age, against spiritual hosts of wickedness in the heavenly places."*

Evil wants us to take the bait, to be angry and resentful, to get offended—because when we get into negative attitudes and feelings, we lose sight of God. Don't let a person who has hurt you also cause you to lose sight of God! A refusal to forgive is like taking poison and hoping the other person will get sick. Forgiving another is for *our* sake.

It takes trust and discipline to keep a healthy attitude when life isn't fair. We can't change the imperfect things that happen to us, but we can choose our attitudes and responses to the injustices of life. We need courage to face the days when we are treated unfairly; wisdom to know whether to fight it or to make the best of it; and serenity to forgive. God uses our pain to accomplish His good in our lives. Answer the following questions in regards to people you have not forgiven:

- Do you carry toxic poisons in your heart and mind all day in the form of resentments and anger?

- Are you willing to do whatever it takes to heal, to get things right, and to be free from the dysfunction, no matter how uncomfortable the process is?

Forgiveness involves cleaning up our own lives by making amends. God tells us to fix things first with the people we've wronged, then come to Him. (Matthew 5:24) He wants us to set our own wrongs straight whenever possible, right away, as long as in doing so, we don't hurt others in the process.

When we begin to see how God has turned around our own lives, even though we have wronged others, we will be able to forgive the people who have wronged us. God wants us to release our guilt and reconcile our relationships. (As noted earlier, it is important to keep in mind that if you have been in a harmful relationship, you can totally distance yourself from it while also forgiving your abuser. Forgiving him does not mean restoring your relationship with *him*, but with *God*.)

It's important to follow the demands of forgiveness instead of our emotions. We can choose whether to be bitter or better. God forgives us so we can forgive others. If you owed someone a million dollars and they said, "Just forget it . . . I forgive you your debt," would you turn around and make someone else pay the $20 she owed you?

When we decide to live by doing the next right thing, we learn to not let our emotions run wild and dictate our actions. In time, our feelings will catch up with our right-acting decisions. Don't be derailed if your feelings don't match up with the action of right-doing. **Forgiveness is not a feeling. Forgiveness is a decision to act a certain way**. It is a choice. When we do it, it breaks the power of evil. Romans 12:21 tells us that we are to overcome evil with good.

God, knowing our weakness as human beings, knew we would need a constant source of forgiveness flowing both to and through us. We all fall short at times. Without God's promise of continual forgiveness, we would soon be weighed down, unable to step ahead. Instead of leaving us encumbered with the heavy burden of missing the mark (sin), He offers us an unending source of forgiveness to lift us up time after time.

Ephesians 4:32 says it in this way: ". . . I need forgiveness so I am going forgive. I need mercy, so I am going to show mercy." In Luke 23:34, we read that, with spikes in his hands and feet, a crown of thorns on His head, his back having been beaten with the Roman scourges, Jesus said, *"Father forgive them; for they do not know what they do."* Forgiveness is about a decision based on the love of God. With Christ in our life, we can do what He did. Jesus is the ultimate forgiver.

It is possible to forgive even somebody who did horrible things to you when you were a child. A very human reaction is, "I want to hurt him like he hurt me" or, "If I can't get justice, I still want revenge" or "I want God to punish him and put him in hell, not heal his life and make him whole."

Forgiveness does not require us to pretend that something never happened. Forgiveness is not about forgetting. It is about letting go of another person's throat. For you to forgive, release the person to God and allow God to redeem him.

We may have to declare our forgiveness for another person a hundred times the first and second day, but by the third day it may be less, and so on, until one day, we realize that we have completely forgiven that person. Then we can pray for his/her wholeness and give them over to God, so that God's love will burn every vestige of corruption from his life.

Forgiving the Unforgivable

Some of us have someone in our past who perpetuated such wrongs on us that, in all earnestness, we cannot find it in our hearts to forgive that person. Maybe you had a perverted father or neglectful mother who turned on you or who looked the other way while another adult abused you. Maybe intellectually you know to forgive, but when you try, you keep seeing pictures of the sexual, mental, and/or physical abuse perpetrated on you as an innocent child.

Maybe it was a romantic interest in adulthood whose hurtfulness you can't face. Whatever the case, consider that all of us started off as children and that we bring the experiences and beliefs we acquired as children into adulthood. While some of us bring a lot of love and understanding from happy, nurturing childhoods, others, who lacked love early on, may bring hate, violence, addiction, shame, guilt, etc.

Every abuser started off life as a little child. Try, if possible, to locate a photo of your abuser when that person was a child—the younger, the better. If you can't get a photo, find a picture of another child that might closely resemble the person you have in mind. As you look at the photo of this innocent-looking child, consider the thought: He/she wasn't born as the monster he/she became! Something very abusive must have happened to him/her to turn him/her from that sweet little child into the adult they became.

Dig into their past. If possible, try talking to various relatives or friends, and see if you can discover what he/she suffered in their early life to change them into the sick person they became. You may find a genuine heartfelt compassion for him/her, and it will be very healing.

Forgiveness doesn't mean we have to let that abusive person back into our life, and it doesn't mean we condone what they did. Forgiveness means *giving up the hope that the past could have been any different from the way it was.* If you have spent a lifetime wishing your past had been different, realize this is not only useless, it is another form of insanity. Forgiving, letting go of the past, and letting go of guilt, are essential to allowing God to heal us. So when old stuff comes up and you want to act out in response to your memories, instead, ask yourself: Am I going to be an unconscious slave to the past or a conscious servant for God?

- In the space below write down some of the wrongs you have made in your life that God has forgiven you for:

_____

_____

_____

_____

_____

_____

Forgiving the unforgivable is an enormous challenge. The willingness to change how we feel about the person who hurt us is essential to healing ourselves and finding the ability to forgive the unforgiveable. Meditate on the Scriptures found at the end of this chapter and learn what God has to say about forgiveness.

Our natural human tendency is not to forgive, so don't expect to wake up one day and think, "Wow, I feel like forgiving today." When we forgive, we give up our right to strike back at the one who hurt us. It's not the world's way, but it is God's way.

Make a decision to forgive. God has already told us to do so. Our forgiveness is not dependent on the other person admitting to their wrongs. Even if you will never see them again, you can forgive. Forgiveness is between you and God.

Once you make the decision to forgive, consider committing to praying daily for the well-being of the person who hurt you. You can decide right in the middle of your pain that, with God's power, you will let it go. Matthew 5:44 tells us to pray for those who hurt you, to bless them in Jesus name.

Write down a simple prayer of blessing or wellness for the person you are choosing to forgive. Below is an example prayer:

Dear God,

I lift up_____ to You, that You would touch their life and bless him/her with health, love and Your presence. Amen.

You won't necessarily feel any better toward the person you forgive at first. You may even doubt that you really forgave them, since you didn't feel differently. But if you have made the decision to forgive, then you *have* forgiven, regardless of your feelings. Write down the date and time you began praying, so you can remind yourself what you chose to do, and observe how you feel as time goes by.

One way to help you forgive wrongdoers in your life is to give yourself what they couldn't give you. Let them off the hook. They can't live up to your expectations, but you can. Remember: You need to make amends to the person you hurt the most—yourself. Decide that each time you give yourself something you need or want, you are forgiving your wrongdoer and improving your life, one day at a time.

Forgiving, making amends, and being free from guilt opens the door to receiving God's promises. Strife will shut the doors to receiving God's best. When we pray for our enemies to be blessed, it will help us to get over our frustration and anger. Forgiving another allows *us* to stop wasting our time being offended by somebody who doesn't even know or care that we are still hurting! It can take a while to get these hurts out of our thoughts, but by refusing to dwell on them, and by deciding not to repeatedly dredge up all the details, we can forgive faster. Forgiveness is a process of making a decision and sticking to a mindset.

Maintaining Forgiveness

How do I maintain forgiveness? Try using the acronym Q–TIP as a key to maintaining forgiveness for those who have wronged us. Q-TIP stands for Quit Taking It Personally. We can rise above taking offense personally. When people wrong us or do evil things, there is often something much bigger behind their actions—something much bigger than us and our egos. Anger or hatred will blind us to the truth of what is actually happening. If we are going to see things accurately, we must see through and operate in the fruits of the Spirit, which are love, patience, tolerance, and self-control.

When we are criticized, we need to try not to defend ourselves or retaliate against the criticism. When we retaliate, we don't solve the problem; we compound it by becoming like the one who hurt us. When we are unjustly criticized, we don't need to be offended; we can know that the truth will eventually come out. It is possible to defuse the power of the offender's criticism by simply replying, "You could be right," or, "That's interesting!"

Think again about Jesus's example: He looked down from the cross at His tormentors, without wrath or retaliation, but with mercy, and prayed, *Father forgive them; for they do not know what they are doing."* (Luke 23:34)

He was not waiting until He came again to get even. He forgave them. He knew they did not understand what they were doing. They lived in a darkness that could not be penetrated without the power of the sacrifice He had come to make for them. He did not come to condemn the world; it was already condemned. He came to save it. He has commissioned us with that same purpose. If it is to be accomplished through us, we too, must lay down our lives and learn not to take offense.

Turning the other cheek to a personal affront is never easy; it was not even easy for Jesus. Even the hope that we may be able to die a little more to our self-will will not give us the strength to endure. Hebrews 12:2-3 declares that there is only one way for us to suffer injustices in the right spirit, and that is by: *"...fixing our eyes on Jesus, the author and perfecter of faith, who for the joy set before Him endured the cross, despising the shame, and has sat down at the right hand of the throne of God. For consider Him who endured such hostility by sinners against Himself, so that you may not grow weary and lose heart."*

God wants us to rule over our own spirit, and it takes self-control not to get offended or angry every time somebody doesn't do what we want the way we want it done. Self-control is needed over our thoughts, our words, and our feelings.

Questions to Answer:

- How have you harmed yourself?

- Are you willing to pray daily for the people who have wronged you so you can be free of resentment?

- How do you become willing to make amends?

- How will making amends release your resentments and shame?

- How does your unwillingness to forgive others block your progress and hurt your relationship with God?

- Why is forgiving yourself an important factor in the amends-making process?

Scriptures Related to Chapter Eight:

Luke 6:27-31	1 John 4:11-12	Ephesians 4:32
Luke 6:37-38	Mathew 6:14-15	Mark 11:25

Prayer for Chapter Eight:

Dear God,

Help me to forgive as You have forgiven me. Fill my heart with the willingness, compassion and love I need to do this. Thank You. Amen.

NINE

Making Amends

Make Amends: Let God lead you to right past wrongs so that you don't have to hide from anyone. Fix what you can without hurting anyone in the process. (*Matthew 5:23-24*)

The work of Chapter Nine will release us from many of our past resentments. Now we make amends to ourselves, our inner child, and to others. We face our mistakes, admit our wrongs, and ask for and extend forgiveness. This work is our means to serenity through fixing whatever we can, without hurting anyone else in the process. It is especially important to use discernment and to seek God's wisdom as we take this step. Making restitution is hard work, but if we skip it, we won't find the freedom we seek. It is after the work in Chapter Nine that we start to see the fruits of the Spirit bloom in our lives: kindness, love, patience, peace, joy, gentleness, and self-control.

In this chapter, we confront issues from our past that may not have been addressed for a long time. We need to reflect carefully upon the amends we intend to make, giving sensitive thought to the appropriate time and place and the form our amends will take.

We make direct amends whenever we can. This can be scary because we are facing unknown outcomes; but we learn to turn those outcomes over to God, trusting that He will be with us, regardless of what happens. Making amends helps us accept the consequences of our past behaviors and take responsibility for the impact our actions have had on others. If someone is unable to receive our amends, we must accept that they are part of the problem and that the situation will have to remain unresolved for now. Our only responsibility is to make a sincere effort.

Making amends is different from simply making apologies. When we apologize, we express regret for a fault or offense. An apology doesn't require a change in our behavior. While still using, I apologized over and over for the same mistakes without ever changing the behavior, thoughts, or feelings that caused the harm in the first place. An amends requires *action*. I must improve, correct, or alter whatever needs to be changed in my behavior. For example, when we apologize for being late, it does not "mend" our tardiness; it only explains or excuses our behavior. Appearing on time is the changed behavior that constitutes amends for habitual tardiness.

The process of making amends is important to our future because it helps us resolve and put aside all distractions and obsessions about the past, allowing us to focus and live in the present. We use this opportunity to repair past wrongs, which allows us to feel good about our efforts to replace misery with serenity. The passing discomfort over confronting our past is nothing compared to the increased self-esteem and acceptance this process brings.

God's peace and true love are like doves that land softly and subtlety. The harsh terrain of fear, anger, and resentments can deflect the landing of peace and love in our souls. Carrying unfinished wrongdoings in my heart keeps me from being at peace with myself and laying my head down on the pillow for a good night's sleep.

As I worked on the list of people I had harmed, I remembered something I had done that no one currently in my life knew about. Even the person I had harmed had lost track of me years ago. But I knew what I had done, and I did not feel at peace about it.

Twenty years earlier, I had been financially bankrupt and couldn't pay my rent and immediate bills. A friend of mine, a doctor, offered to lend me a few thousand dollars to catch up and get by. She generously told me I could pay her back slowly in small monthly installments. Shortly after accepting her loan, I moved to another state and conveniently lost touch with her. I rationalized that, because she was financially secure, she wouldn't miss the money. Over the years, when the thought of this kind person entered my mind, I quickly turned my attention to other things.

Recovering requires self-honesty. That meant being completely honest with myself before God. I knew I could no longer sleep with any wrongs I had swept under the rug. If I wanted to feel clean and clear in my heart, I would have to clean and clear my past. As I reluctantly put this woman on my list, I debated in myself whether it would really be necessary to contact her. I let myself think about how difficult it would be to pay back this large sum of money. But the truth was that never paying her back was wrong. It was time to make this situation right, even though I was again in difficult financial straits.

I found the woman's current address and wrote a letter, telling her I was now in recovery from addictions and apologized for not having made good on my promise, years earlier, to repay her loan and her kindness. I explained that, as a single mother, I was still not financially stable, but said I could start sending her fifty dollars a month, promising to increase that amount as soon as possible. I enclosed my phone number and address with my first payment and mailed the letter.

The old "entitled victim" had the thought, "Maybe she'll be happy enough that I tried to make amends, and, since she has plenty of money, she'll release me from this financial obligation."

A week later, I received her response. She accepted my apology and was glad to hear about my recovery. She explained that she, too, had had some financial hardships, due to a recent illness, and that she would appreciate every penny paid back as soon as possible.

Over the next year, I made her my financial priority. Any time I received extra income, I put it into my payments to her. By the end of one year, I had paid her off. It was a major feat for me, and the spiritual benefits I received far outweighed the financial strain and sacrifice this reparation required.

Completing this amends created a sense of integrity that began to replace the sense of shame I had carried from past abuse. You can't buy integrity. Integrity is about how you act when no one is looking; it is doing the right thing when no one else knows about it. Integrity grows and develops through practice. There is no greater peace and fulfillment than that which comes from making this kind of amends in recovery.

At this point in our recovery work, we are gaining peace and a new sense of freedom. We're discovering that the horrible things that happened to us are now our experience, strength, and hope— they are the very things God uses to help others. Through practicing these recovery steps, we are gaining an interest in others, and we no longer dwell in self-pity or live without purpose. We are beginning to lose the need to get what we want, when we want it, the way we want it; instead we seek to serve God and others. Instead of feeling alone and isolated, we are connected. We know that God is in charge and will not leave us stranded or abandoned. We are learning that, with God's guidance and provision, we can get through whatever challenges we face.

As we make amends, we cease fighting ourselves and others. We begin to understand our part in the problems we have had, and to know that God can change our lives. We learn to refrain from jumping into unhealthy and dangerous relationships. We recognize that God is doing for us what we have been unable to do for ourselves on our own.

We came to recovery to deal with our relationship issues and were told to pursue God. But how do we pursue God? We follow and apply in our daily lives the spiritual principles discussed in these chapters. We focus on ourselves, our thoughts, choices, feelings, and behaviors. We receive God's help in developing our character as He removes our defects. The miracle is that, by the time we are making amends, sanity has returned and we are recovering. (If this is not, in fact, what you are experiencing, don't despair! Just thoroughly rework the previous steps to see what parts of the work you omitted or skimped on.)

Making Amends to Ourselves

Getting into unhealthy and/or abusive relationships, acting out within those relationships, using addictions, picking the wrong partners, putting a relationship before God, and putting ourselves in dangerous situations—all these behaviors contributed to the harms we suffered. As we make amends to ourselves, we look at how we can change those behaviors in order to correct the wrongs we have done to ourselves.

Making amends to ourselves for these harmful behaviors is the key to moving forward spiritually. We do this by practicing true repentance. Repentance, like amends, does not mean just saying, "I'm sorry; I won't do it again." It is the act of learning and practicing new behaviors as we turn away from old behaviors and do things differently.

Most of us have been unable to love ourselves, to forgive ourselves, to protect ourselves, to be ourselves, and to be kind to ourselves, because we have not known how. We can waste time today, asking, "Why have I been like this?" Or we can, instead, spend time asking, "What can I do to change and make this right now?"

The decision to forgive ourselves is not just a statement. Rather, it is the actions of forgiveness. When we forgive others, we extend kindness, consideration, and understanding. In just that same way, we must turn this same forgiveness inward toward ourselves. When we truly forgive ourselves, we behave differently, extending to ourselves the same love, care, and kindness we offer others we forgive.

Where we have hurt ourselves repeatedly by dwelling on guilt for past behaviors, now we make a living amends by accepting what has been and by acknowledging that we did the best we could at the time. (Even if we *knew* better, we still did not know how to *do* better.) We make a choice to view our past differently and to acknowledge that God will use our wrongdoings and our previous mess as a means of helping and inspiring others who are struggling through what we have come through. God will turn our mess into a useful "mess-age"!

As we've discussed, many of the harms in our past occurred because we voluntarily placed ourselves in abusive and dangerous situations. We did this because we did not know how to protect ourselves; because we did not know how to speak up and use our voices to take a stand for what was appropriate for us. We were afraid we would lose the people in our lives if we resisted what they wanted. We sacrificed ourselves to become what someone else wanted.

Now, as we make a living amends to ourselves, we learn to provide safety and protection for ourselves through God's guidance. We set boundaries and we communicate clearly to others about what we consider to be acceptable and unacceptable behaviors. This boundary-setting requires stating what the consequences will be for violating our boundaries, and then consistently enforcing those consequences. As we learn to trust God and to let go of the fear of what others think and feel, we slowly lose the fear of abandonment. We will see that, if someone leaves our side because they're not willing to respect what is healthy and right for us, it is better that they go on their way.

One area in which we begin to make amends to ourselves is in our love lives. We look at who we are dating and consider whether that person is safe, healthy, and appropriate for us to date. It is important that we change the questions we ask about the man. Now, instead of looking at *his likes*, we consider *our needs*.

Here is a list of questions a healthy person will ask herself in the early stages of dating. The answers to these questions might raise red flags about continuing to date this person. Truthful answers to these simple questions, early on, can help you to avoid a lot of heartache and drama later on:

- If you became sick or injured, would he help you and be there for you?

- How does he react when life doesn't go the way he expected?

- Does he have a temper?

- Does he work hard and is he disciplined?

- Is he emotionally available or does he disappear in response to your emotional needs?

- Would you like to see your daughter date the kind of man you're dating?

- Does he tell the truth and is he trustworthy?

- Does he answer your calls promptly?

- Does he get mad at your personal requests, or does he enjoy pleasing you?

- Would he rather be right or happy?

- Is it more important for him to argue his point of view or to understand how you feel and what you're asking?

Another change we can make is to identify, before we even begin to date, what a godly man looks like. Most of us know that making amends and changing our relationship behaviors require us to draw on what we are *learning*, not on what we have lived. Consider the following questions:

- Would a godly man be someone who is confident in himself and has a secure sense of purpose?

- Would he be someone who is close to God, and knows the right priorities, which puts God first in his life?

- Would he exude honesty and respectability because of his service to others in his community?

- How do you think this kind of man would treat the woman in his life?

- Would he treat her as an equal partner, be supportive of her endeavors, and not feel threatened by her achievements?

- Would he hear her needs and respond with care because he knows God's love personally?

- Would he enjoy giving, loving, and blessing his wife, and would he recognize her as a special gift in his life, because God brought them together?

- Would he honor her and his commitment to her through all kinds of challenges, and would be her best friend?

- Would he protect her, romance her, and ultimately be willing to lay down his life for her?

Now, wouldn't that kind of man make for a good and lasting relationship?

To help you develop some healthy, higher standards for a good man in your life, make a list of the godly qualities you desire in a mate. While no one is going to fit the whole bill perfectly, it's important to have a standard, a level of conduct you will expect in anyone you date. In Column 1 below, I have written down some examples of qualities found in a godly man. Let my list spur your imagination to write out, in Column 2, the qualities *you* want to find in a godly man.

Ex. Qualities in a Godly Man: **Qualities I Want in a Godly man:**

Has integrity.   _____

Places God as first priority.   _____

Loves and obeys God.   _____

Is competent.   _____

Is disciplined.   _____

Is wise, kind, and loving.   _____

Reaches out to others.   _____

Is honest.   _____

Is faithful and trustworthy.   _____

Is true to his word.   _____

Is committed.   _____

Endures the test of time.   _____

Is filled with humility.   _____

Is stable and hardworking.   _____

Is a good listener.   _____

Keep this list as a reminder of the character traits and qualities that are now part of your new, higher standard of dating choices. You deserve to be treated well. Knowing that, and standing firm for that, is part of making a living amends to yourself in relationships. You can only love someone to the degree to which you have allowed yourself to be loved by God.

Sex is another major area in which we can change our behaviors and make amends to ourselves. How we behave sexually will determine how well we learn to protect ourselves and set ourselves up to succeed. Dating is the way to get to know someone. The hope is that, by building a deep and caring relationship with the right person, we can achieve a permanent union through the commitment of marriage.

According to God's design, sex is supposed to be a *byproduct* of love and intimacy, not, as many people seem to think, a means of *creating* love and intimacy. That's putting the horse before the cart. We make a huge mistake when we focus on experiencing physical-feel-good moments and bypass the necessary steps of building a relationship, first.

As we date, we progress through the peaks and valleys of everyday life, and emotional and spiritual intimacy deepens. Then, when dating leads to marriage, we can attain physical oneness. Our sexual relationship is the ultimate sign of our oneness in God's eyes, the physical symbol of our complete, spiritual union.

Spiritual and emotional intimacy, established first, better prepares us for deeply satisfying and meaningful sexual intimacy in marriage. Jumping into bed before knowing the person well and establishing a deep spiritual connection, first, is trying to build a relationship backwards. Are you willing to change your dating behavior? Are you willing to connect spiritually, emotionally, and intellectually first before experiencing a sexual relationship? If so, your relationship will be built on solid ground that will eventually support your physical union.

Having sexual intimacy early in a relationship puts us in harm's way. For most women, making love means investing a huge part of herself in the other person. The act of physical intimacy is intertwined with the urge to connect and make a home. Most men, on the other hand, are innately pursuers and hunters. If we have sex before a deep relationship develops and a real commitment is made, we take away one of the main reasons a man will pursue a commitment to begin with. Women naturally want to commit, but often men need a reason to do so.

Sex distorts clear judgment. It can cloud our perceptions of who we're sleeping with if we get sexually and emotionally invested too soon. Instead of staying objective and focusing on whether this person is right for us, we focus on sex and getting a commitment out of the man—whoever he really is!

You may ask, "What does all this matter, as long as I really care about the person I'm sleeping with?" There are spiritual principles that, applied to a relationship, will set you up to receive God's best. God is love, and He wants us to be treated in loving and appropriate ways. He established for us a code of conduct—not to say, "Here are the rules and you need to live by them, whether they work for you or not," but because these spiritual principles answer the human need for emotional security. These are not so much *rules* as they are God's revelations to us about how the human soul functions at its very best and healthiest. They nurture our understanding of God's fidelity. By working through our issues with each other, we glimpse the fidelity of God.

Changing behavior often means undergoing the discipline of not doing what my mind and body want to do. Don't let your urges lead and govern you, or you can pay a high price in the end. Your life depends on thinking straight when you're deciding with whom to get involved and what to do in a relationship.

Sometimes the healthiest thing to do, if you decide you may be getting involved with the wrong person, is to cancel a date or not make a phone call. Don't let yourself slip backwards and settle for someone you know is not right for you just because you don't want to experience the loss of somebody or feel abandonment in the moment. Today, we can choose to opt out for short-term satisfaction and choose instead, a long-term victory. Allow the temporary feelings of emptiness and loss to wash over you. They will pass. When you wait on God, He will give you more than what you could have imagined.

These living amends also protect us, while dating, from the perils casual sex can bring. Dangers like STD's (Sexually Transmitted Diseases), genital herpes, HPV, and HIV are incurable, and AIDS can lead to death. Abstinence from sex is one way to avoid all of those hazards. Abstinence is also the only 100% reliable method of birth control. No other method can guarantee safety from pregnancy or disease; each one has a failure rate. By following God's direction for sexual relations and abstinence, we can successfully diminish or eliminate a lot of unwanted problems in our lives. There are sound reasons for following God's advice for sexual relations.

Casual sex can take a toll on us spiritually and emotionally as well as physically. But no matter what our sexual histories are, it is never too late to start over. We can't get our *physical* virginity back, but God can give us a fresh, new start by giving us a clean heart along with our *spiritual* virginity. You can, spiritually, become a virgin again. Some people call this second-time virginity. All we need to do is ask for forgiveness.

Nothing is too big for God to forgive. We have no need and no excuse to carry shame about our past sexual activities any longer. God can restore our spirit to us. 1 John 1:9 tells us, *"If we confess our sins, He is faithful and just to forgive us our sins and to cleanse us from all unrighteousness."* Christ will forgive and cleanse and free us from the effects of all our past sexual encounters.

If you are dating someone, or when you start dating someone in the future, and sexual advances are made, tell your man "plain and simple" that you've made a commitment to sexual abstinence until and unless you marry; that you are doing it God's way. If he's the one, he'll help you remain true and committed to your Heavenly Husband, first and foremost. If the man rejects you because you want to stay pure, then he isn't interested in building a relationship

God's way, he doesn't truly love you to begin with, and he is not the one for you. You don't need someone like that in your life.

We need to let go of our preconceived ideas, and trust God. Don't compromise yourself in order to end up with less than what you started with: Hope. We already have all we truly need with God. A good, tried-and-true man in a relationship is icing on the cake. Whatever we compromise to keep a man, we're going to lose anyway. So do what's right for *you*. Following God's lead protects your heart, your life, and your future.

Consider officially making a written commitment to being a virgin and not having sex until marriage. Psalm 37:5-6, 9, says "*Commit your way to the LORD, trust also in Him, and He shall bring it to pass. He shall bring forth your righteousness as the light, and your justice as the noonday . . . But those who wait on the LORD, they shall inherit the earth.*" Read the following commitment carefully, and then consider signing it:

I, _____, have learned that sexual abstinence is God's way of protecting me from heartbreak, regrets, disease, abuse, and an unplanned pregnancy. I will save my heart and my body for that special person of God's choosing.

I repent, and ask for and receive God's forgiveness. I accept being given a new, clean slate in God's eyes. I know God has a good plan for my life and I will not let past memories shame me into believing I have a hopeless future. I am a new person and will act accordingly.

I pledge that I will wait until marriage to have sex, knowing that God will bless that union and my decision to be faithful to Him!

_____   _____
Signed   *Date*

Making Amends to Your Inner Child

What if the little child in you is hurt, afraid and buried? It is up to us to make amends with that part of ourselves. It's up to us to learn to re-parent and heal our inner child. Until we get into recovery, our inner child stays wounded and cut off from us. Many of us have spent most of our time surviving, with no energy left over for exploring creativity. God wants us to become like little children again. Making amends to ourselves means letting go of fear and self-consciousness. It may mean playing, going outside in the fresh air, smelling the flowers, writing a poem, or singing a song. To explore our creative side, we must get past a fear of looking foolish or trying new things.

The Bible tells us that faith pleases God and that we are to have childlike faith. (Hebrews 11:6) Children don't worry about what they'll eat for lunch three days from now, or whether their parents will provide them a room to sleep in two weeks from now. And we're not supposed to worry about those things, either. We're to live in certain faith that God will meet all our needs. (Matthew 6:31–33) Our key to everything is: Seek God's Kingdom, first and foremost, and approach Him as little children asking to come in. (Matthew 18:3)

So part of our amends to our inner child is to develop and bring out our childlike qualities: spontaneity, honesty, innocence, trust, fun, and creativity. Children are very much like God, especially in their joy in creativity, which is a part of God that dwells in each of us and encompasses all the childlike qualities mentioned above. Getting in touch with our inner child will cause our creativity to flow! It's important to set aside some time every day to be creative. Being creative is part of living a balanced life for God.

Many of us never had any hobbies, were creative, or even felt driven toward a career. We seemed to lack the passion other people had. But passion and creativity are born into each of us. When our childhood is stolen from us, we don't get a chance to develop that, but that doesn't mean we don't have it. Our hearts' desires just get buried under the struggles to survive everyday life.

As we make amends to our inner child, we must be kind, gentle, and patient as we try new things. We must let go of being afraid of making a mistake, of not being liked, or of not being ourselves.

It's never too late to become a kid again—or for the first time! Whether the child in you has suffered wrongdoings imposed in childhood, or harm from your own choices in adulthood, making amends to your inner child is part of the process of this work in Chapter Nine. Recapturing the little child in us is part of the process of becoming whole and healed. We can learn to play and have fun. Take some time and watch children play. They are naturally enthusiastic, excited, light-hearted, inquisitive, and joyful. Let a child teach you how to play and have fun, or look over the list below and try doing some of the many things that can bring out the child in you:

Walk
Dance
Sing
Get a massage
Have a sauna
Take a bubble bath
Go to a movie
Go to a concert
Visit an art gallery
Go to garage sales
Listen to music
Play an instrument
Play cards
Draw a drawing
Paint a picture
Take photographs
Write a poem
Take a country drive
Go to the theater
Visit the flea market

Ride a horse
Play racquetball
Play tennis
Play golf
Go to the beach
Look for seashells
Fly a kite
Go roller skating
Go sailing
Go swimming
Go sun bathing
Go fishing
Go camping
Hike in nature
Ride a bike
Go skiing
Take a sleigh ride
Make a snowman
Go to the zoo
Go canoeing

Browse in a bookstore	Take a trip
Go metal detecting	Pack a picnic
Visit a friend	Pick flowers
Decorate a cake	Plant flowers
Bake some cookies	Smell the roses

There are endless possibilities. There's purpose and accomplishment in having fun. Don't feel guilty, thinking you're wasting time! Time is never wasted! Play and joy feed the child in you! Everyone has the potential to feel passion. If you haven't found yours yet, you'll find it—by playing!

Ask yourself, *If all you really have is this moment, why aren't you doing what is truest to your heart? What would life be like if you lived true to yourself?*

Making Amends to Others

As we prepare to do this part of our amends, we refer back to Chapter Eight's list of the people we harmed. As we now approach the people we are going to make amends to, it is important to let go of pride and to have a helpful and forgiving spirit. We must also be willing to refrain from criticizing, accusing the other person, or defending ourselves. The main purpose for making amends is to clean *our* side of the street; therefore, we do not look to discuss the other's faults.

As we prepare to make amends, the more we pray and open our hearts to God ahead of time, the better our chances of saying the right thing when the moment comes.

If you are calm, honest, and open through the encounter, you will be grateful for the experience. It is best to keep your statements and explanations simple, without rehashing details. Often, the other person will thank you for your effort at amends. But their response, and whether they accept your intention of amends, should not matter in the end. This is strictly about you doing the right thing. Before making amends, do an attitude check by answering the following questions:

- Are you willing to love and forgive yourself and the person to whom this amends is to be made?

- Are you taking responsibility for your part in the situation? Will what you say, and how you will say it, reflect this understanding of your part in the problem?

- Are you staying focused on your part not the other person's part in the situation?

- Are you devoting some prep time to prayer and meditation?

- Are you willing to turn your fears and anxieties over to God?

- Are you willing to do more inventory work if you're angry or upset and are delaying the amends?

- Do you know what you want to say, and will you be careful not to blame the person with whom you are communicating?

- Are you keeping your statements simple, since details and explanations aren't necessary?

- Are you willing to accept the consequences of this encounter, whatever they are?

- Are you willing to resist expecting a specific response from the other person?

When thinking about making amends to others, we see that there are some people we can approach easily (Right Away), others we may not be able to have direct contact with right now (Some Time), and some with whom we may have to defer action (Never).

Before we actually go to make our amends, it can be helpful to write down some thoughts about what we might say. This can help us stay focused in a situation that might feel stressful and unsettling to us. What follows is an example to consider and change to fit your own needs or situation:

I was _____ *(ex., scared, overwhelmed,*
feeling abandoned, etc.) when _____
(the occurrence) happened between us.

I ask your forgiveness for _____ *(the*
specific harm done) and for any other way in which my thoughts,
words, or actions have caused you pain.

I would like to make up for what happened by: _____

_____

_____

(Describe what you could do to atone for the harm you caused.)

Will you accept my amends?

With some idea in mind of what we will say—and having prepared ourselves through prayer, meditation, guidance, and an attitude check—we set off to attend to those on our "Right Away" list.

We first ask the person's permission before making our amends. We can say something like, "I am following a program that requires me to be aware of the harm I have done to others and to take responsibility for my actions. I'd like to talk with you about the damage I caused you and our relationship and what I might be able to do to make things right between us again. Are you willing to talk with me about this?"

If it is possible to make an active restitution—repaying money we owe, for example—we can ask the person's permission do so. Some people may refuse to be reconciled, despite our best efforts to make amends, and the situation may not change. Luke 6:27-36 teaches us about keeping our side of the street clean, saying that we no longer need to be controlled by other peoples' actions and reactions.

A "Some Time" amends might include someone I don't know how to find; or it might include a situation for which this might not be the right time and place for making my amends. In that case, I turn the matter over to God and pay close attention: If He presents me with the opportunity to make amends to a person on my Some Time list, I go ahead and do so.

The last category, our "Never" amends, includes two situations: people who are no longer accessible, and situations in which making amends could cause further harm to them or to myself. A "Never" amends would include someone who has died, for example—someone it simply is never going to be possible to make my amends to, at least not in this life. The second situation will require careful thought, prayer, and conversation with a caring mentor, for it involves deciding whether someone could actually be harmed by my making amends. It would be wrong and hurtful, for instance, to "make amends" by telling an unsuspecting wife that I had slept with her husband. I might end up feeling relieved by that confession, but only at the cost of the other person's well-being, which would be totally outside the intent and purpose of amends. I can make indirect amends for any infidelity or promiscuity by changing my behavior or by helping another person who has been betrayed and cheated on in the way I had cheated or betrayed another.

Someone already in poor emotional or physical health might also belong in the "Never" category. Likewise, it is unwise to approach someone who continues to be harmful to our mental or emotional health and/or to our physical safety. In a situation in which we could be at risk, indirect amends are recommended. We can once again make such amends by helping others who suffer as we did.

Two other means of making indirect amends include: praying for the person on our "Never" list; and writing a letter we will never mail. In such a letter, we "talk it out" as if we were actually communicating with the absent person. This can be particularly helpful when we need to make amends to one who has died.

Indirect amends can also be made by doing a special kindness for someone else's child or parent when we no longer have the opportunity to do it for our own relative. We can make important amends to our adult children by respecting their adulthood and maintaining our own recovery as healthy adults, both physically and emotionally. Many times, we make amends by how we live today. A living amends is made through our choice of a healthy lifestyle.

Our mentors can help us evaluate each situation and come up with useful, appropriate indirect amends for everyone who truly belongs on our "Never" list.

One of the great benefits to us of making amends is finding that we are no longer held captive by our feelings or by the feelings of others. By choosing to forgive and by acting in loving ways, we can be free from control by anyone other than God. As we forgive others and do good, our feelings begin to change. Peace comes as we let go of our attempts to defend and vindicate ourselves.

As we lay down all our injustices, received and given, and place them in God's hands for His resolve, it is easier to forgive those who have wronged us and to be forgiven for our part. As we make amends, fears and insecurities diminish and we find the safety of God's protection around us where we could not protect ourselves. Slowly, little by little, as we seek the higher spiritual road, God's peace and presence increase in our lives.

Questions to Answer:

• Who on your amends list causes you the most anxiety?

• Who on your amends list do you consider to be an enemy?

- What expectations do you have for how other people will receive your amends? Check your motives.

- What sort of changes or restitution are you willing to undertake to set right your wrongs?

- Are you letting God and a program of recovery guide you in making amends?

Scriptures Related to Chapter Nine:

Matthew 5:23-24   Ezekiel 33:15-16   Romans 13:8   Philippians 2:3-4
1 Peter 4:8-10   Luke 6:35-36   Romans 12:17-21

Prayer for Chapter Nine:

Dear God,

I ask for Your strength, guidance, and direction to do the right thing, and for willingness to accept the personal consequences of my past wrongdoings. Help me to seek and pray for other peoples' happiness, and give me discernment about who, when, and how to make my amends. I pray that I will put aside any self—pride, and trust in Your help and in the counsel of others. I ask that You would show me Your ways of patience, tolerance, kindness, and love as I seek to clean house. Thank You. Amen.

Keeping the Peace . . .

A contented mind is the greatest blessing
a man can enjoy in this world.

—Joseph Addison

Steps 10 and 11 are designed to keep us in fit
spiritual condition by keeping our house clean and
seeking communication and guidance from God.

Maintainance

Maintain: Accept that you will make mistakes. Make daily spot checks and, when you mess up, fix them as soon as possible. Continue to trust and obey God so that you can maintain the changes He makes in you. *(1 Corinthians 10:12)*

Chapter Ten work starts the maintenance part of our recovery. We take a personal inventory daily and aim at setting right any mistakes we make as we go along. By now, we realize that working a spiritual program of recovery is a lifelong journey done one day at a time, and that we need to continue to clean house. This understanding enables us to relax into the never-ending process and to stop trying to "finish the program."

A Chapter Ten Check-Up can be used in two ways.

When we feel restless, irritable, and discontent, we stop and look for any evidence that our own selfishness, self-seeking, dishonesty, and fear are at work, dragging us backwards into old self-destructive behaviors. We want to figure out what is going on in our lives. Chapter Ten's Check-Up is basically a mini-version of the work in Chapters 1-9, now applied to a particular issue. Once we see our part in whatever the problem is, we promptly admit our wrong, share it with another human being, ask God to remove it, and make prompt amends for our part.

This Check-Up is also used to look at ourselves, at the end of

each day, and to make adjustments in our behaviors where necessary. Again, we look at ourselves, see our errors, promptly admit
them, and make corrections. Doing this regularly helps us to more
readily identify and use our strengths and to spot and handle our
weaknesses. We need to accept that we are imperfect human beings
who will mess up.

Over the first ten years during which I took care of my father
before he died, he criticized and verbally attacked me unmercifully
daily. He had a way of offending and hurting me that brought me to
my knees. In my pain, I cried untold tears when I left his presence.
My emotional sobriety and peace were continually challenged and
shaken. I knew I needed something to change in order to continue
caring for him while still maintaining some peace of mind.

On one typical day, everything that could go wrong, did. As the
day progressed, I began to feel as if I were in quicksand and sinking
fast. My elderly father's dementia, combined with his often harsh
and judgmental attitude toward people, frequently led him to make
offensive remarks about others. To my horror, he did just that, that
afternoon, in his doctor's waiting room: He deeply offended three
people with unkind comments about their appearances. Being hard
of hearing, he thought he was whispering when he was actually
shouting and was easily heard by everyone there.

On leaving the doctor's office, we went to return a pair of shoes
he had insisted on buying the day before and now did not want.
But the shoes were not returnable because the store was going out
of business. Dad was sure they were *not* going out of business, but
were trying to steal his money. He made a scene with the store manager, refusing to take no for an answer. I finally slipped a note to
another sales person with a second check, asking that they pretend
to refund my father's money so that we could resolve the matter
and leave.

On returning home, I found mail from one of the state agen-
cies that helped pay for my mother's nursing home expenses. They
were terminating some of the financial aid because of something
I had supposedly failed to do. I knew this was mistake because I

always stayed on top of the paperwork. But solving the problem required spending the next two hours on the phone, either on hold or transferred repeatedly—to the wrong people. Eventually, I was told I needed to get a certain form filled out again, since it had probably gotten lost in the mail.

Just when I thought I couldn't get any more stressed, my father insisted that the pharmacy had not given him the right number of pills. Two were missing, he said, and he flew into a rage. Nothing I said or did calmed him until, finally, I noticed two pills on the floor next to where he was sitting. They must have slipped through his arthritic fingers, unnoticed, while he was counting out the pills.

By that evening, I felt drained, irritable, and upset. I couldn't stop crying. I wanted to eat, or drink, run away, or just throw in the towel. In my desperation to feel better, I began looking at the steps we've worked on in Chapters One through Nine to see how they could be applied to my specific issue of reacting to my father and letting his behaviors get the best of me.

To start with, I admitted I was powerless over his thinking and attitudes, and that our interactions were causing me emotional unmanageability. (Chapter One's Powerlessness)

I made the choice to believe God could restore me to peace, even in this situation, and that God had the solution. (Chapter Two's Belief)

I turned my father and my feelings over to the care of God and His will. (Chapter Three's Decision)

I recognized my resentment and fears over my father's behavior and how they brought out the worst in me as I reacted to him. (Chapter Four's Inventory)

I saw that my part in this problem was how I took his verbal attacks personally and expected him to act differently. I was needing him to be the kind of father I had always wanted him to be, and not accepting him for who he actually was. I recognized that he was not only spiritually sick, but that he too was a wounded child who acted out. I began to see that he was not capable of acting the way I wanted him to, that my wants were like expecting to have a sophisticated, intellectual conversation with a two-year-old. He did not know how to give the emotional, loving intimacy I craved from him. As I spoke about all this to my mentor, myself, and God, I realized that my part was to let go of my expectations toward my father's behavior. (Chapter Five's Telling It)

I needed help in not reacting to him and not habitually dwelling negatively on what he said. I needed to be ready to let go of my old ways of thinking and acting. (Chapter Six's Preparing)

I asked God to change me. (Chapter Seven's Asking for God's Help)

I looked at how I had harmed my father, instead of at how he had harmed me: I would lose my temper as he tried to push me around; I would get mad at him back. Mostly, I saw how, in my early years, I had hurt him indirectly by living an unstable life, all the while reacting to his dysfunction and continuing to blame him for my shortcomings as an adult. (Chapter Eight's Making a List)

I realized that, no matter what my father did to me, I could still make my amends to him for how I had lived before recovery, and how I had reacted to him, by taking care of him that very day. My living amends would be to be the hands and feet of Christ to him. Jesus did not defend Himself or take offense to those who knew not what they did. (Chapter Nine's Making Amends)

For the first time, I had a higher calling attached to the challenges of taking care of my father. Chapter Ten's Check-Up showed me how this experience could be an opportunity to practice and develop patience, tolerance, and unconditional love toward my father. By doing a mini-spot check inventory on an issue that affected my peace during the day, I was able to see my part and change so that I could become a better person.

By attending to fears and resentments that crop up daily with the people I interact with, I am able to keep my side of the street clean and not let the emotional garbage accumulate to the point of needing a complete overhaul. Instead, a daily sweeping will keep the front porch clean.

The key to a Chapter Ten Check-Up is recognizing right away when we need to do it. A review keeps us focused on today instead of worrying about the future or living in the past. It is like the inventory work of Chapter Four, except, here, we are concerned only with today. The review is usually brief and can be done at any time during the day or just before going to sleep. Here are a few questions to regularly ask ourselves before bedtime so as to maintain peace and spiritual health. These questions help us live the recovery program in all areas of our lives:

- Was I restless, irritable, or discontent?

- Did I have trouble with personal relationships?

- Was I unable to control my emotions?

- Did I fall into misery and depression?

- Did I feel useless or unable to be of help to someone else?

- Was I full of fear?

- Was I unhappy?

- Was I resentful, dishonest, self-seeking, or afraid?

- Was there something I needed to discuss with someone, but didn't?

- Was I kind and loving toward everyone I came in contact with?

- Was I thinking of myself most of the day, instead of thinking of what I could do for others?

- Do I owe anyone an apology?

- Is there anything I could have done better?

- Did I try to manipulate people to get things to go my way?

- Was I honest and true to myself, or did I seek to please others, instead?

- Did I act out with self-destructive behaviors?

- Was I feeling different, alone, and not talking about my feelings?

- Was I accepting and forgiving, letting go of former resentments?

- When I was wrong, did I promptly admit it?

- Did I run my day on self-will and self-reliance, or did I surrender to God's will and ways?

- Did I judge or criticize myself or someone else harshly today?

- Am I remembering that I can ask for help and that I can call someone?

Spot Check Inventory On Fear

When you lost your peace and serenity because you were fearful, ask: What am I afraid of?

Then identify your behavior from the choices below:

        ❑ I am being *self-reliant.*
               or
        ❑ I am being *God-reliant.*

Spot-Check Inventory On Resentment

When you've lost your peace and serenity because of a resentment, ask: What am I resentful about?

Then pick one of the following answers:

> ☐ I will lose what I have.
>> or
> ☐ I will not get what I want.

These questions and your answers can help you identify where you are in your own personal will/worldly thinking, and where you need to exchange it for God's ways and thoughts. To get back on track say aloud God's promises, addressing your fears and/or resentments. You can refer to **God's Promises for Well Woman**, found in the Appendices in the back of this book. If you are caught up in your emotions and unsettled, call your mentor or trusted friend for help, a listening ear, and some suggestions. And if you have offended, angered, or hurt someone, make amends as soon as possible.

Old thoughts, feelings, or behaviors can knock at the door of our hearts and minds on any given day, at any given moment. By spotting the thought that brought up the feeling that caused us to act inappropriately, we can take prompt, corrective action and admit our wrongs. Every day, throughout the day, take thoughts captive. We need to be careful not to become worried and fearful because doing so diminishes our usefulness to others.

After making our Check-Up review, we ask God's forgiveness and seek His guidance for what corrective measures should be taken.

We can assess our weaknesses, as we review our day, by using the following check list:

Personality Characteristics of Self-Will
Where Have I Been:

Selfish and Self-Seeking	Intolerant
Dishonest	Resentful
Fearful	Hateful
Inconsiderate	Destructive
Prideful, In Self-Will	Impatient
Greedy	Wallowing in Self-Pity

Angry	Defensive
Envious	Self-Condemning
Lazy	Suspicious
Gluttonous	Doubtful

Chapter Ten's work is not just about looking at what we've done wrong and fixing it. It is also about looking at what we've done right. Since many of us are blinded to the beauty inside us, and do not realize the assets we possess, look at the following list and circle as many attributes as you can, including those you would like to have in your life:

Personality Characteristics of God's Will

Where Have I Been:

Interested In Others	Balanced
Honest	Tolerant
Compassionate	Forgiving
Courageous	Loving
Considerate	Disciplined
Creative	Unselfish
Humble	Seeking God's Will
Modest	Open-Minded
Generous	Faithful
Peaceful	Trustworthy
Grateful	Patient
Motivated	Willing

Then, after circling your assets, sit quietly and affirm each one to yourself by repeating:

"I am _____ (fill in the asset)."

"I am _____ (fill in the asset)."

"I am _____ (fill in the asset)."

Being Content

Many of us did not learn in childhood how to handle our emotions. Without consistent direction and discipline for our toddler-like temper tantrums, we have learned to let our emotions run our lives. So we may need to learn *now* what we should have been taught at age two regarding what to do when something triggers deep-seeded emotions.

We can't let our feelings become our master. We have to ask ourselves whether we're bowing down to our feelings and letting them control us, or whether we are following the Word of God. There is no magic wand that can make life's messiness and our humanness disappear.

The Apostle Paul faced horrible challenges throughout his life, and yet he learned to be content in every situation he found himself, no matter how difficult. (Philippians 4:11-13) The world trains us to think that external circumstances cause our inner disturbances, but Paul's life teaches us that, with God, we can be at peace *regardless of* our circumstances. In recovery, we call that *acceptance*, which brings with it the serenity we are seeking.

When we feel panicked, disturbed, or can't think straight, we don't have to stay in that agitated state—there is a way out. We can make a decision that we're unwilling to live without peace. We'll have to work at it by paying attention to what triggers us. Ask yourself, "What sends feelings of abandonment whirling in my head, stirring up my fears?" Then tell yourself the truth: "You are never alone! God is always with you!"

The last thing Jesus gave us before He departed was His peace! (John 14:27) Not only are we capable of feeling peace, but God *promises* us a sound mind. (2 Timothy 1:7) Lay claim to God's promise. Make it your job to be one who *". . . dwells in the secret place of the Most High."* (Psalm 91:1) When we dwell in God's secret place of prayer, faith, and action, we can stay calm in the midst of a storm. Meditate on the four scriptures following:

Philippians 4:11-13   2 Timothy 1:7

John 14:27   Psalm 91:1

Speak them back to God every time you feel challenged by fear, instability, and emotional turmoil. God promises that we can be content in all things. He has not given us a spirit of fear, but of stability and a sound mind.

Recovery and spiritual principles tell us that we should do as we *know* not as we *feel*. We may *feel* that we have no self-control and we may not *feel* capable of having peace, but we already have it! When we turned to God and prayed to have Him come into our life, He placed a seed of self-control within us, and His peace He gives to us. It is up to us to nurture it through practice, over and over again. When we are restored to relationship with God, seeds of the fruit of the spirit—love, joy, peace, forbearance, kindness, goodness, faithfulness, gentleness, and self-control—are planted in us. (Galatians 5:22-23) The seeds of the spirit give us the choice and ability to become different.

Abiding in the peace of God is a great spiritual weapon that evil has no power against. Paul wrote in Romans 16:20, *"The God of peace will soon crush Satan under your feet."* Most oppressive attacks upon believers are intended to first rob them of their peace. The peace of God is the first foundation of the fruit of the Spirit; it must be in place to hold all of the others in place. Once we get anxious and fretful, it's easy to lose sight of God's will in our lives. Once we lose the peace of God, we can quickly lose our patience, love, self-control, etc. Overreacting to offenses and opposition from people can rob us of our peace. If we are rooted in Christ, we will not be intimidated by even the most severe challenges or offenses.

Matthew 5:9 tells us, *"Blessed are the peacemakers, for they shall be called sons of God."* And we read in Luke 1:79 that Christ came to *"... guide our feet into the way of peace."* For this reason, we should ourselves see if we are indeed growing in this "way of peace." Christ was even called the "Prince of Peace" (Isaiah 9:6), so, as His representatives, we are to become examples of this peace. It needs to be one of our primary characteristics.

Worry and anxiety are not fruits of the Spirit, and the Lord cannot lead us if we allow them to dictate our state of being. God makes His peace available to all who come to Him. Are you going to follow the Spirit and abide in the fruit of the Spirit, which is: "... *love, joy, peace, patience, kindness, goodness, faithfulness, gentleness, self-control"*? (Galatians 5:22-23) Or are you going to allow worry to dictate the course of your life?

If we choose God's way, we can rest in His promise found in Philippians 4:4-7: "*And the peace of God, which surpasses all comprehension, shall guard your hearts and your minds in Christ Jesus.*"

We must learn to quickly recognize anything that is attacking our peace and trying to steal it. We can resolve that every time our peace is threatened, we will use the experience, instead, as an opportunity to strengthen our serenity.

The peace of God is rooted in trusting in Him. We have peace because we know who He is and who He rules over. We trust His authority and know that nothing can touch us unless He allows it. We trust Him to know that anything He allows is for our good, as He has promised in Romans 8:28: "*And we know that God causes all things to work together for good to those who love God, to those who are called according to His purpose.*"

We can have peace, even joy, in everything, including during our trials, because we know that He will cause everything to work for our good. The true successes of our lives are dependent on trusting in God and living a surrendered life to Him and His ways.

Anger

One of the fastest ways to lose our peace is to act out in anger. Hurting people hurt others. It is a vicious cycle. Anger feeds off itself. When we are attacked by an angry person, we tend to attack back, which only perpetuates the anger. We find our thoughts going 'round and 'round about the angry *this-for-that* exchanges we've had! It is helpful to remember that anger usually arises from a person's fear and pain. If we can pause long enough to remember that, it will help us stop reacting to anger with anger.

Chapter Ten asks us to take responsibility for how we feel and what we do with our feelings. Many of us believe happiness comes to us through someone or something outside ourselves. Likewise, we think we are unhappy because someone or something else made us feel that way, too. The truth is, our feelings are determined by our thinking. We can stop reacting to others as though our happiness and peace are subject to their behaviors.

Victims say things like, "You hurt my feelings," or "You make me feel bad," and "You make me mad." But other people don't have the power to *make us* feel angry. No one can *make* us feel anything we do not allow, accept, and generate within ourselves. Still, it is true that our feelings do not happen out of the blue. The key to managing our anger is figuring out which of our needs are not being met by a situation, and by then taking care of them, ourselves.

Anger is like a smoke alarm. It tells us something is wrong. Rather than reacting badly to it, we can use it as a warning—to identify our need in a situation—and as a signal that we need to meet that need. Since anger, hurt, and disappointment result from unrealized expectations for how our needs should be met and who we think should meet them, ask yourself the following questions to identify your unmet needs:

- Why am I angry?

- What do I really want?

- What need/desire of mine is not being fulfilled?

- How can I meet that need now, myself?

Once we have determined what our need is, we must do what we can to meet it, knowing that when we do the possible, God does the impossible. He will see to it that people willing to support our

efforts cross our path—so be open to the people and opportunities that present themselves. When we take charge of our lives,
we free everyone else from the impossible responsibility of taking
care of us, and we free ourselves from the need to be angry at
someone else.

Our needs can be met when we partner with God to meet them.
Hebrews 4:16 tells us, *"Let us then approach God's throne of grace with
confidence, so that we may receive mercy and find grace to help us in
our time of need."* (NIV) You are a daughter of a King (God) who
owns everything. All you have to do is petition Him, do your part
(whatever He guides you to do), and leave the rest to Him. Looking
to God, who is sovereign over everything, means we are linked to
unlimited resources and that nothing is impossible!

It is unrealistic, impossible, and inappropriate for us to assign a
person in our life the sole job of anticipating and meeting all of our
needs. The slogan "Let it begin with me" reminds us that no one
is a mind reader. We must remember that our needs today are met
by God, and partner with Him. Even though our needs as children
weren't met, we don't have to fear not having them met now.

Another aid to dealing with a person who continually brings up
anger in us is to focus on the positive qualities of the person we are
angry at. If we concentrate on the other person's mistakes, we'll
find them and make them grow, and we'll see that person through a
negative lens. If we look for and affirm the constructive qualities in
that person, then we'll see our relationship with him or her through
a positive lens. (Matthew 7:3-5) What we dwell on will contribute
to the memories, feelings, and attitudes that set the course of our
interactions in the future. Choose to view people through God's
eyes. It takes practice, but God gives us time to get it right.

An appropriate response to others can also neutralize our anger.
When someone continually says things that bother you and pushes
your emotional buttons, learn to verbalize what you need. Whenever possible, communicate what you're feeling. Accusatory remarks
like *You made me feel . . .* or *You're wrong* or *That's not true* break down
communication and get people on the defensive. But when you use

statements like *I feel* . . . or *I think* . . . or *I believe* or *I want* . . . you're letting others know your perspective without blaming them. Share your experience; ask what their feelings are, and then listen. We can build bridges between ourselves and others by learning about them, or we can build walls by trying to be right. Since we all seek to be understood, if you want to neutralize a potential argument, try saying, *You could be right!* Could you continue a fight with someone who says, "If I were you, I'd feel that way, too!" ?

Most of us like to talk about ourselves and explain/defend our views. Did you ever consider that the time you spend talking is the amount of time you are not learning anything new? If we spend more time questioning, listening to, and finding out about the other person's views, we will learn more. Try asking yourself, "Why am I talking so much? Don't I already know what I think?"

Getting to know someone better, so that a deeper quality of friendship can grow, can help us learn to love the imperfect people in our lives. The following list of questions can help you learn more about others in your life:

• What stressors is this person dealing with right now?

• What are some of this person's dreams and goals?

• What are this person's spiritual beliefs and values?

• How kind and respectful am I to this person?

• Do I appreciate the things this person does in our relationship?

• Do I consider his or her needs?

• Do I take time and enjoy talking with him or her?

• Is there a lot of give-and-take in our discussions?

- Do I agree to disagree and listen respectfully to him or her?

- Do I seek his or her help and advice in problem-solving?

How well we get to know someone depends on our willingness to listen to their answers without taking a defensive stance. When we are defensive, we close down our ability to hear, and communication ceases.

In order to stop attack-attack-back exchanges, stop arguing and agree on some guidelines for talking out disagreements. We need rules! When we play a board game, both people have to understand and agree on the rules of the game before playing. We can't make up the rules to *Monopoly* as we go along. And when it comes to arguing, we need to agree ahead of time with the person on behavior parameters that we'll adhere to during an argument. Those will be our board game rules.

The rules for arguing are to be no different from the rules of chess, checkers, and other games. Recognize that we have two goals in talking through a disagreement. The first is to understand the other person's point of view, not to convince them to change theirs for ours. The second is to find a creative solution we can both live with. If we seek to please the other person and give as much as we can, it will come back to us! To accomplish your goals, set up rules ahead of time. The following is a list of rules you can adapt and apply to your relationships:

Rule One: *When one of you is talking, the other needs to listen with no interruptions.* Listening means you hear what the other person is saying about his experience, thoughts, and feelings. Then you share yours.

Rule Two: *Keep the focus of your statements on yourself,* using "I" messages, rather than using "You" messages when you speak. "You" messages imply blame. Don't judge each other. Look for similarities in what you each desire.

Rule Three: *When you feel hurt or angry and want to attack through words, respond neutrally* with statement like, "I don't see it that way, but I can understand how you might." Don't introduce your views with blame-and-attack statements like, "You waste all your time on your interests and ignore me."

Rule Four: *Watch your tone.* Learn to persuade and influence rather than demand and direct. Listen for your partner's tone of voice, too, and if it comes across negatively, take that as a signal that the request is important to him.

Rule Five: *When all else fails, exit the argument.* Ways to exit a futile argument include: changing the topic to something completely unrelated and upbeat; taking some time to tell each other about the things you love and appreciate in each other; taking a twenty minute break, agreeing to talk again when you are both calm. If a stalemate still persists, agree to turn the disagreement over to God and pray together for God to work it out.

Rule Six: *Don't tolerate bad behavior,* especially in the beginning of a relationship because it will set the future tone. Keep your standards of acceptable behavior high.

As you go along, you can add or adjust rules to suit your relationship's needs.

A set of rules can give us a methodical way to set boundaries and turn fighting into a fair and constructive dialogue. It can provide a sound way to negotiate solutions and a roadmap for navigating the treacherous terrain of arguments.

Sometimes, someone can really set off our anger and we may become too emotional to have a balanced discussion. When that happens, try writing to the other person. It's a good method of communication when we're feeling too emotionally volatile to speak face-to-face about what we're feeling. Writing can help us express our points in a healthy, not hurtful way. Sometimes writing is the best way to clearly convey our needs while staying neutral and positive.

Back Up Card

Finally, know that mistakes will be made—by the other person, as well as by you. When the offending person comes to you, apologizing, offer yourself and them an opportunity to backtrack using a Back-Up Card. In essence, the Back-Up Card is a free pass to redo a mistake and to remember the truth that God gives us endless Backup Cards through His grace and mercy. What we have freely received, we can pay forward to others. This is what a Back-Up Card looks like:

Back Up Card

I love _____ (name) and _____ (name) loves me.

I forgive _____ (name). I will allow him/her/myself to step back, start over, and do the right thing.

I will remember that forgiveness means having to say you're sorry **only once!**

Controlling your emotions, forgiving others, and allowing them second chances, is how God wants us to learn to love others. Don't let the everyday stuff that happens between you and others steal your serenity. Stop going around in circles. We can do our part, and God will do what we can't do.

When you feel shaky and your emotions rise to the surface, determine not to overreact. Quietly remind yourself: *God planted the seed of self-control in me, now grow it!* Believe you can act maturely. Pause before saying anything. Count to ten. Don't say anything at all until you can express your feelings and needs appropriately and constructively.

The minute you decide you're going to stop reacting when your emotional buttons are pushed, you'll probably have lots of opportunities in your life to test your new resolve. Be prepared to practice what you've been shown! Know that it is possible for anyone to attain emotional sobriety. As we practice, using the tools of recovery, we can achieve control and maturity in our feelings and reactions. Remember: You are responsible for deciding how you act. To stop acting out, learn to be quiet and pay attention to the Five Watches:

> *The Five Watches:*
> *Watch your thoughts. They become words.*
> *Watch your words. They become actions.*
> *Watch your actions. They become habits.*
> *Watch your habits. They become character.*
> *Watch your character. It becomes your destiny.*

Accepting God's Will and Timing

Our job is to keep our side of the street clean by doing the next right thing in our lives. The rest is up to God; He determines the outcomes. We are merely actors in His play here on earth. He's the director and author of our lives. When we live in His Kingdom, we don't have to continue waiting for the other shoe to drop. God doesn't throw shoes at us!

We can stop comparing our life today to what it was. We're no longer who we used to be, and we can expect new and different outcomes. When we live in God's Kingdom, things turn out differently because Christ is involved. We don't know what God has up His sleeve. Stop continually trying to figure God out. More will be revealed on an "as needed" basis. Ecclesiastes 3:1-8 talks about and elaborates on divine timing:

> *To everything there is a season, A time for every purpose under Heaven: A time to be born, And a time to die; A time to plant, And a time to pluck what is planted; A time to kill, And a time to heal; A time to break down, And a time to build up; A time to weep, And a time to laugh; A time to mourn, And a time to dance; A time to cast*

away stones, And a time to gather stones; A time to embrace, And a time to refrain from embracing; A time to gain, And a time to lose; A time to keep, And a time to throw away; A time to tear, And a time to sew; A time to keep silence, And a time to speak; A time to love, And a time to hate; A time of war, And a time of peace.

Don't question and fear an unknowable future. Instead, trust it to a known God. Absolute obedience demonstrates your trust in God. How do you act while you're waiting on God? Are you grateful to God in all things?

We strengthen our patience when we give God control of our lives and decide to live according to His timetable. If we accept what happens to us, and trust God to use for good what was meant for harm, we are able to keep our faith even in the most trying experiences. Spiritual growth is slow; only weeds grow quickly. Acknowledging powerlessness builds the patience to persevere with what we can do and the faith to leave the results to God. The truly faithful remain steadfast even when times become hard.

Impatience is one of the biggest stumbling blocks to receiving God's best. From fast food to fast pace, our culture resists patience. If a promise of God doesn't come to pass in six months or less, don't give up. Scriptures teach that anything that comes too fast or too easily can be insignificant. Great men of the Bible had to wait years before seeing God's promises come to pass. Moses spent forty years in the wilderness before God called him. Paul the Apostle waited in the wilderness for some fourteen years before getting his message from God. Joseph spent years in jail, waiting on God's fulfillment in his life, and David spent years running for his life and hiding out before he was made king.

Truly faithful people remain steadfast when times become hard and temptations are strong. The more obedient you are, the more your trust in God is demonstrated, the more victory, growth, and peace you will have.

As we learn to give up control, we begin to reduce our stress levels. Since nothing happens by chance and without God allowing it, acceptance is the key to our problems. Matthew 10:29-31 says, *"Are not two sparrows sold for a copper coin? And not one of them falls to the ground apart from your Father's will. But the very hairs of your head are all numbered. Do not fear therefore; you are of more value than many sparrows."* Once you identify your resistance to accepting what is (*accepting*, not necessarily liking!), then you can try praying:

> *Dear God,*
> *Help me to want what I have. Amen.*

God always gives us what we need, not necessarily what we want. Wants create stress. Stress comes from wanting what we don't have. Sometimes what we want would not serve our best interest in the long run. Since God sees the bigger view of our lives, we can learn to trust and be grateful for not only what we do have, but what we *don't* have.

The root of most of our stress is in wanting things to be different. Some tension and stress is good and can motivate us to do whatever is required to bring about good changes. But when we can't get what we want and it's out of our control, remember we only have control over our self, our attitude, and our actions. To keep our serenity, we may need to put our desires into God's hands and trust in the goodness of His ultimate outcome.

Give God the chance to bless you the way *He* wants to. God doesn't do shortcuts. We all feel vulnerable to uncertainties and fears, but by doing things our way, and out of sync with God's timing, we can create a lot of unnecessary problems in our relationships and our life. God knows better than we do what we need. Often, we're not ready for what we request, or what we ask for is not what we need. By trying to make things happen ourselves, prematurely, the best of what God has to offer is pushed aside. Many of our challenges are allowed because they prepare us and develop us spiritually.

Often, we complicate our own lives and get in God's way when we interfere in the lives of others through controlling, manipulating, enabling, and assuming responsibility for their life lessons and challenges. It's important to identify what our responsibility really is, in regard to other people and the relationships in our life. We need to figure out whether our "good intention" to help someone we love is actually a disguise for enabling the other person and therefore hurting both of us. Maybe the other person's problems are not supposed to be ours. When seeking to determine whether we were helping someone or enabling them, ask the following questions:

- Are the people or persons I'm helping infecting me or being affected by me?

- Are they sucking the life energy from me because they don't want to change?

- Am I caught up in thinking that being a good person means trying to fix them and help another person, no matter what?

- Have I been so busy helping and fixing them, I've denied God Himself the opportunity to touch and rescue them? Have I tried to get them to work out their mess with me instead of with God?

- Can I let go of trying to do what will make me temporarily feel better now, so that, later, I can feel better with lasting results?

- Do I want the pain of discipline now or the pain of regret tomorrow?

If we live as if God is completely in control and will really do what He promised, we won't live in fear.

THE SERENITY PRAYER AND THE GOD BOX
The first part of the Serenity Prayer is a great tool for letting go of fear, trusting, and partnering with God. It is used in many 12 Step recovery programs. It reads:

"God, grant me the serenity to accept the things I cannot change,
Courage to change the things I can,
And wisdom to know the difference."

—*Reinhold Niebuhr*

This prayer can become our filing system for the issues in our life. It can help us determine what we need to do, what we don't need to do, and how to tell the difference. For those things we can't do anything about, we have a God Box, and all the things we cannot change or fix, we put there for His care and resolution. Below is an adaptation of the serenity prayer. Fill in its blanks regarding your present concerns:

God, grant me the serenity to accept the things I cannot change . . .
 (I can't make _____ [name the person] do what I want.)

The courage to change the things I can . . .
 (I can change my thoughts and the way I feel about myself.)

And the wisdom to know the difference . . .
 (I can have peace and know <u>what to do</u> or <u>not do</u>.)

Now that you've identified what or who is out of your control, remember that God can do anything. Nothing is too hard for God. He is the ultimate "Mr. Fix-It." We may not have been able to lean on our earthly parents, but we can lean on our Heavenly parent for the strength, courage, and wisdom to deal with the hard things in life. Let God handle what you can't.

When our path appears blocked, God sees a way around the block. God can carve a path through any problem. Through faith, put it in His hands and leave it alone until and unless further instructed. Creating a God Box can help us do this. Psalm 55:22 tells us, *"Cast thy burden upon the Lord and He shall sustain thee; He shall never suffer the righteous to be moved."*

So get a container or box in which you will store your challenges. Whenever you are experiencing a challenge, or are faced with a fearful situation, write it down on a piece of paper and place it in your God Box. Say the following prayer as you write down your problems and put them into your Let-Go-And-Let-God Box.

Dear God,

Once again, I find myself feeling helpless over a situation. I've been trying to fix it, but, if anything, I've only made it worse. I am writing down my problems on this paper and putting it in my God Box as a symbolic means of handing this issue over to You. I am letting go of this problem and leaving the solution to You. I believe that when I occasionally check what is in my God box, I will find that some things in it are no longer problems. Amen.

Remember: God will listen to you (Psalm 145:18-19), God will continue to defend you (2 Chronicles 20:17), and God will never reject you. (James 4:8 and Psalm 94:14)

If you find yourself worrying and fretting over the issue again, remove it from the God Box. Only put it back in once you have decided to put it back in God's hands.

Every few months, clean out your God Box. Throw away the problems that have been resolved. You will see how God continues to take care of your prayers for His help and how He transforms your fears and concerns into blessings, over time, as you take your hands off of what is not yours to fix.

Now that we've identified what we can't fix, and we've prayed for acceptance and put the problem in God's hands to resolve, we can begin to focus our thoughts on God's promises.

We live in a world that contradicts everything God says. By focusing on the hope found in God's Word, we can live above our circumstances and know joy in the midst of hardship. Joy is the knowledge that we will have something good. To be joyful is to know God's promises and trust in His outcomes. God is love and He is good. God's authority reigns over everything, and He is sovereign.

While we are waiting on God to do His part, we can do our own part by believing what He says. God promises us a new life as He heals and renews our minds and emotions through His Spirit and His Word. He offers us hope, peace, honor, protection, and love in exchange for our past sins and misery. While there are thousands of promises found in the Bible, a few that are key and lifesaving are listed in the Appendices in the back of this book under **God's Promises for Well Women**.

Questions to Answer:

- What actions do you take daily so as to continue to experience recovery?

- When do you need a Spot Check inventory?

- List an example that shows you are relating better to others.

- Cite a recent situation in which you did not behave appropriately. What did you do when you realized you were in error?

- How does taking a daily inventory support your spiritual growth?

- How does correcting your wrongs save you from unnecessary consequences?

Scriptures Related to Chapter Ten:

1 Corinthians 10:12	Ephesians 4:22-28	Hebrews 12:14-15
Psalm 34:12-14	James 1:23-25	Philippians 4:4-7

Prayer for Chapter Ten:

Dear God,

Grant me Your peace. Help me guard my heart and my mind; help me watch for selfishness, dishonesty, resentment, and fear. When I recognize that these have surfaced, I pray that You would remove them so I can better do Your will. Thank You. Amen.

ELEVEN

Prayer and Meditation

Pray and Meditate: Seek contact with God through prayer and meditation. Let Him, who is greater than you, show you how to live and guide you through life. *(Colossians 3:16a)*

While Chapter Ten Check-Ups help us keep our house clean, the work of Chapter Eleven is about seeking and following God's will. We need to remember that our real purpose in life is doing God's will and staying in touch with Him through prayer and meditation. Using this practice, we seek throughout the day to know God's will for us and the power to carry it out. It is the means by which we reach God and experience God reaching us. This habit also enhances our intuition, which is often the vehicle through which God's wisdom flows to us. Guidance comes to us from His spirit to ours, and as we learn to trust God and live in alignment with His will, we can reap a life of hope, love, and victory!

While prayer is a way of talking directly with God and of requesting guidance and knowledge of His will in our lives, meditation is a way of listening to God and calming our minds, ridding ourselves of daily, worrisome thoughts and concerns so that we can hear God's guidance and will for us.

My mind had always been a playground for negative thoughts. If someone did or said something that upset me, I could dwell on that until, before long, negative thoughts were running amok in my mind, playing and re-playing like a skipping record spinning round and round on a turntable.

There are times in a relationship or in a situation where the right thing to do is *nothing*. These are times when we must wait on God, when it is best not to act, think, or talk. Until recovery, I had no idea how to control my thinking or refrain from acting on my feelings. I was impulsive, and I spoke too quickly. I said things I soon regretted and did things rashly, without weighing the possible consequences of my actions.

My mind was like an untamed stallion. I needed some way to restrain my thoughts and reactions to the people and situations that pushed my buttons. When I first began to practice meditation, I tried to stay focused on one specific thought for only five minutes at a time. I was aghast at how slowly each minute passed and how difficult it was for me to maintain my focus. I had to continually force myself to let go of intruding thoughts and go back to the focus thought.

Doing this mental discipline was not fun, and I wanted to quit. But I didn't. I continued the practice of meditation daily. The more I did it, the easier it got.

Eventually, my increased "mental muscle tone" began to overflow into my everyday life. When challenges arose in my relationships, I was able to refrain more and more from reacting and to pause, instead, and pray for the next right action. When I became upset with what someone said or did, and I didn't know what the next right thing to do was, I was increasingly able to wait and seek guidance before responding.

Practicing prayer and meditation is an ongoing, regular necessity for me. If I slack off, my mental muscles begin to atrophy. Meditating and praying keeps me centered and poised even in the midst of chaos outside and around me. Today, I am increasingly able to consciously manage and choose the thoughts I dwell on and the feelings I act on. Meditation and prayer are the reins that bridal my mind and emotions, steering me away from negativity, keeping the spiritual airwaves clear for conscious contact with God. Through this practice, my mind and thought-life have become a tamed and trained horse I can ride.

You may ask, "How can I find the time to pray and meditate?" Being too busy can be a big obstacle to increased conscious contact with God and experiencing an intimate relationship with Him. Even if we are running ourselves ragged for the sake of others, we can still jeopardize keeping God first. We need to watch for and limit the amount of unnecessary distractions we allow in our daily lives. Simplify! Avoid the temptations to overspend, or to borrow, and then to have to worry and overwork yourself to pay back your debt. Limit how much time you spend on iPhones, TV, iPods, iPads, and other electronic devices so you don't get used to constant noise and mental busyness, thereby jamming your mind and breaking your connection and communication with God. *Could "BUSY" mean: B-eing U-nder S-atan's Y-oke?*

We live in a world that contradicts everything God stands for. The world teaches that our first priorities are food, then water, housing, career, security, relationships, self-actualization—and, lastly, if there is actually any time left over, God. But God asks us to prioritize in the opposite order, putting Him first. He tells us that, if we do so, all the rest of our needs—where we live, what we eat, and procuring our clothing and other provisions—will be taken care of, just as surely as God provides for the needs of the birds in the air and the flowers in the fields:

Therefore I tell you, do not worry about your life, what you will eat or drink; or about your body, what you will wear. Is not life more important than food, and the body more important than clothes? Look at the birds of the air; they do not sow or reap or store away in barns, and yet your heavenly Father feeds them. Are you not much more valuable than they? Who of you by worrying can add a single hour to his life? And why do you worry about clothes? See how the lilies of the field grow. They do not labor or spin. Yet I tell you that not even Solomon in all his splendor was dressed like one of these. If that is how God clothes the grass of the field, which is here today and

tomorrow is thrown into the fire, will He not much more clothe you,
O you of little faith? So do not worry, saying, "What shall we eat?"
or "What shall we drink?" or "What shall we wear?" For the pagans
run after all these things, and your heavenly Father knows that you
need them. But seek first His kingdom and His righteousness, and
all these things will be given to you as well. Therefore do not worry
about tomorrow, for tomorrow will worry about itself. Each day has
enough trouble of its own. (Matthew 6:25-34, NIV)

Trusting God to order our lives, we can slow down, live, and enjoy God's gifts. Not all the tasks we put on our To Do lists are on His schedule for our day. Leave room for God to guide your use of time and energy. Time spent each day in quiet meditation can give us a glimpse of God's timelessness and we can see that our schedules are not that important when measured against eternity. As God's presence seeps into our awareness, we can relax into the fullness and peace of each moment.

Spiritual rest is a state of peace, contentment, serenity, refreshment, stillness, tranquility, and calm. Spiritual rest helps us learn how to *be* rather than *do*. Often, our ability to wait without impatience increases, and rash impulsivity decreases. Over time, as we consistently practice spending time with God, we become truer to ourselves, we live by higher values, enjoy the moment more deeply, and breathe more easily in life.

Prayer

In Chapter Eleven, we learn how to pray and what to pray for. We learn to ask to know God's will for our lives, trusting Him to know our best interests. The old habit of praying for material things will diminish, replaced with prayers for guidance. We begin to rely upon prayers like the *Serenity Prayer* and the *Lord's Prayer* as models for simple recovery practices.

Praying only for God's will and for the power to carry that out, we are helped to empty our minds of our preoccupations with self, making it more possible to experience God's presence. Seeking God's will humbles us humans, who are so accustomed to running our lives by our own plan and making demands on God to give us what we think we want. If we place our will in God's care, and pray sincerely for His guidance, we find ourselves trusting that our will is being redirected. As we practice this step, we often acquire a deep sense of gratitude along with a feeling of belonging in this world.

Morning Prayer

We can begin our day with a morning prayer that sets the tone for the day, keeps our priorities straight, and steers the ship for the next twenty-four hours. Spiritually, we are given only a daily reprieve from the demands of our addictions and self-destructive behaviors, so our focus in prayer is to renew *each day* our willingness to seek God's will for us.

We ask God to keep our thoughts and actions divorced from selfish, self-seeking, dishonest, and fearful motives, and for freedom from self-will. We are careful to ask to know what will benefit us and others in the process. We ask God for the right thoughts and intuitive guidance for the day and for the strength needed to carry out the tasks of the day and any problems that arise. Then we can relax and just act on the next right thing, based on our intuition, without worrying.

> *Dear God,*
>
> *I ask You to direct my thoughts, motives, and actions that, free from self-will, I may carry out Your will today. Keep me from selfish, self-seeking, dishonest, and fearful motives. Grant me whatever I need to carry out the tasks and challenges of the day so that my actions are beneficial to myself and others. Thank You. Amen.*

Prayer During the Day in Moments of Indecision or Fear

When you encounter fear, anger, doubt, or anxiety in your day, instead of reacting in confusion, pause and pray this short prayer. It is very simple and will keep you focused on doing the next right thing. Relax and breathe deeply several times, then turn the problem over to God.

Dear God,

I ask for the right thought or action here. I know I am no longer running the show. Your will be done, not mine. Amen.

Prayer at the End of the Day

As we end our day, we ask God's help in discerning where we "missed the mark" that day and for guidance in knowing what corrective action we need to take. We learned this practice in Chapter Ten, and now we incorporate it into the practices of Chapter Eleven. Asking for knowledge of God's will for us, we forgive ourselves and ask God to help us learn from our mistakes. We give thanks to God for the direction and blessings that were part of the day.

Dear God,

Continue to reveal Your will for me. Guide me in any corrective actions I need to take, and help me to forgive myself and learn from my mistakes. Thank You for today's blessings and directions. Amen.

Before recovery, many of us only practiced "foxhole prayers". Those are prayers we say when we're desperate, fearfully pleading for God to do *our* will. How many times have you begged, "God, get me out of this..." or "Stop someone from doing this..." or "Make someone do that..."?

Developing a prayer life helps us become more of what we want to be and less of what we don't want to be. When we let our minds run wild and focus on our own wills, we feed the ungodly in us, and insanity ensues. Happiness doesn't depend on what we have or what we do; it's determined by what we think. So learn to think on good things. God tells us in Galatians 6:7-9: *"Do not be deceived, God is not mocked; for whatever a man sows, that he will also reap. For he who sows to his flesh will of the flesh reap corruption, but he who sows to the Spirit will of the Spirit reap everlasting life. And let us not grow weary while doing good, for in due season we shall reap if we do not lose heart."*

Stop reacting in the same old ways to the same old irritants in your life. God's advice to us is to kill the flesh and feed the Spirit within us. Prayer will help us focus on God, tame our mind, feed our spirit, experience peace, and maintain our daily spiritual condition. It will put us in partnership with God.

Our level of sanity and peace each day will be a direct reflection of how sincerely we pray for knowledge of God's will and the power to act on it. There are two prayers that can help us do this. The *Serenity Prayer* helps us acknowledge our powerlessness to change people and situations. We have already read the short version of this prayer, but here it is again:

> *God, Grant me the serenity to*
> *accept the things I cannot change;*
> *courage to change the things I can;*
> *and wisdom to know the difference. Amen.*

The more we use this prayer, especially when we feel out of control, the more we'll remember Who *is* in control. The more we seek His will, the more peace and serenity we'll have in our lives. The only person we can change is ourselves; the rest is up to God. We are to take care of our side of the street and leave the rest to Him. Since nothing happens by chance in God's world, the fastest track back to serenity is acceptance. Answer the following questions:

- How often do you want other people to stop acting in certain ways or doing certain things because of how their behaviors make *you* feel?

- How often is your thinking directed toward getting others to change?

- Do you deal with your unrest and disturbance by blaming and trying to controlling the outside world?

- Are you blinded to your part in things, and never at peace?

- How often do you consider changing yourself instead of others?

The second prayer, the *Lord's Prayer*, God Himself taught us in Matthew 6:9-13. This prayer covers all our needs for provision, protection, and purpose, and helps us seek and know God's will for us today so that we can keep our priorities in line with His:

> *Our Father, who art in Heaven, Hallowed be thy Name.*
> *Thy Kingdom come. Thy will be done, On earth as it is in Heaven.*
> *Give us this day our daily bread.*
> *And forgive us our debts, as we forgive our debtors,*
> *And lead us not into temptation, but deliver us from evil.*
> *For Yours is the Kingdom, and the power, and the glory, forever and ever.*
> *Amen.*

Meditation

When we give God our love and attention, it pleases Him. He wants us to keep our minds on Him throughout the day. His greatest commandment is that we love Him with all our hearts, our souls, and our minds. (Matthew 22:37-38) To love God with **all** our mind means to discipline our minds to focus on Him.

A good tool for training our minds to stay focused on God is the kind of meditation I discussed early in this chapter. Meditation, a state of mind in which we're open, quiet, and receptive, teaches us to quiet our minds. We give our five physical senses a rest and turn our attention inward, away from the cares and concerns of the day. Meditation relieves tension, strengthens self-control, reduces mind chatter, and generally brings greater clarity. With daily meditation, we'll have less fear, dwell less on negative thoughts, and find it easier to have conscious contact with God.

- Is your mind often a jumble of thoughts, as if filled with a noisy committee that meets regularly in your head?

- Is much of your behavior at the mercy of what you think?

- Are you committed to rooting out unproductive or destructive thoughts and their consequences in your life?

- Do you need to learn to quiet your mind?

The hardest thing about clearing your mind is how fast unrelated thoughts pop back into it. When that happens, don't worry. Everyone experiences this as they begin practicing meditation. Acknowledge the "intruder" and then gently guide your thoughts back to God. Shifting your attention is something you already do many times during the course of a day, usually automatically and semi-consciously. So now you are going to do that intentionally and at will, which will decrease obsessive or negative thinking. When fearful thoughts enter your mind, shift your attention back to the promises and solutions for your life.

Have patience with yourself while learning to meditate. If you can't focus at first, don't get frustrated. Through time, perseverance, and practice you will learn to direct your thoughts. As you are better able to master control over your mind and therefore your emotions, you will become better at responding, rather than reacting, to the button-pushers in your life. Aren't you and God worth setting aside twenty minutes a day for?

Below is a simple guided meditation. Get into a comfortable position. The important thing is to keep your spine straight. Let go of expectations regarding your experience, because it is different for every person. Read through the meditation process below, and then follow it, or have a friend read it to you as you practice it the first time:

SET THE INTENTION: Take a moment to know and feel that you are safe and secure. Imagine a white light of warmth and love surrounding you. Imagine that within this light only peace and relaxation can enter. Ask God to be with you now.

TAKE THREE DEEP BREATHS: Focus on your breathing. Take

in slow, deep breaths, filling your stomach first, then raising your diaphragm, and finally inflating your lungs to capacity. Hold the breath for a moment. Then slowly exhale. Repeat this two more times, breathing in slowly and deeply, holding it and exhaling slowly and completely.

Now relax. If you like, imagine these three deep breaths as representing the body, mind, and spirit. With each inhalation, think, "I am breathing in God's light." With each exhalation, think, "I am breathing out negativity."

RELAX YOUR BODY: Close your eyes. Tighten your toes and feet muscles for about five seconds, then relax them. Tighten your calves and knees; relax them. Continue on up the body, feeling the tension in each muscle as you tighten it. As you release it, let go of any stiffness. Imagine all the tensions, concerns, and anxieties leaving your body. Tense and relax each of the following groups of muscles:

Toes and Feet
Calves and Knees
Thighs
Stomach and Rear
Hands and Arms
Chest and Shoulders
Face and Cheeks
Finally, relax all the muscles in your body.

MEDITATIVE FOCUSING: In meditation, we focus on actual words, and those words are God's. Remember that God's Word is a living thing. It is active. It is powerful. And it has the power to change circumstances. So we choose a focus thought—a simple word, or the essence of a phrase or a piece of Scripture. When you notice other distracting thoughts attracting your attention, return your mind back onto your focus thought. Your focus thought will function like an arrow pointing in the direction you want to go.

Let those intruding thoughts—the need to make a phone call or to do the laundry—just flow past you. As long as they are just passing through, you don't need to do anything about them. It's when you get focused on them, and they get a hold of you, that you need to return to your word or phrase and re-focus on just it. At first, this may be challenging, but as you practice retraining your mind, your ability to do this will grow.

Choose a focus thought like I AM AT PEACE. Begin to softly repeat it aloud to yourself. I AM AT PEACE. . . I AM AT PEACE . . . I AM AT PEACE . . . Now begin to whisper this to yourself. I Am At Peace. . . I Am At Peace . . . I Am At Peace . . .

Then silently focus on your thought: I AM AT PEACE. . . I AM AT PEACE . . . Do this for about ten to fifteen minutes. You can keep a clock nearby to check your time.

FOCUS YOUR ATTENTION BACK TO THE 'HERE': When you are ready to end your meditation time, begin slowly bringing your attention back into the room. Become aware of your hands, your feet, and your body. When you feel ready to return to your normal waking state, slowly open your eyes and begin to move around. Take a few minutes to readjust.

This meditation practice may take only five or ten minutes, and yet you may feel as if an hour has gone by. Regular practice can help you feel centered and relaxed from head to toe. Below is a brief reminder of the steps in this process. Use this form to guide you into meditation at any time during the course of the day when you feel stressed.

1. Ask for God's presence and protection.

2. Breathe deeply.

3. Relax your body.

4. Focus on a thought or word, i.e. *blessed* or *joy* or *love* or *peace*.

5. Return your attention to the "Here."

We practice prayer and meditation so that we can improve communication with God. We know and experience peace, love, and victory when we surrender our lives to God's love, care, and guidance. The benefit of prayer and meditation is an increased ability to determine, live by, and carry out God's will for us.

So how can we tell what God's will is for us? That, of course, is an important question, often difficult to answer with total certainty. But we do know that God does not create confusion and chaos. God is not in a rush and He is never defeated or unfaithful. Our God is a God of order, love, peace, patience, hope, mercy, healing, and restoration. He is sovereign over everything. He owns it all and He is on our side. He wants us to succeed and to come to Him and trust Him. He promises to protect and guide us. When faced with making a decision or choosing a course of action for which you seek to know God's will, answer the following questions:

- Are you making the decision out of fear?

- Are you anxious, pressured, or rushing to decide this because you are invested in wanting what you want, regardless of what God's will might be?

- Are you avoiding asking God for His guidance?

- Are you unwilling to let time and unfolding events show you what you need to do?

- Have you forgotten that you've asked God to block you from going down a path that does not serve His will?

If you answered *yes* to any of the above questions, you might be in self-will instead of God's will. Often, if you are anxious and in a hurry, it is a sign you are seeking your own way, based on fear. To get back on track, living in faith and seeking God's will in your choices and actions, consider looking at what your intentions and priorities are:

- Are you anxious because you want what you want—now?

- Are you afraid that if you give the matter to God, you won't get what you want the way you want it?

- Can you ask God to help you trust Him in this situation?

- Can you ask God's direction and guidance so that you can clearly, intuitively receive it?

When we are not clear, it is wise to do nothing and let time take care of unfolding events. Sometimes, life gives us the clues that "more will be revealed," and we eventually receive information that enables us to make a better choice.

Sometimes God guides us using the people in our lives. We may hear the same words spoken by two separate and independent sources, and know that the words ring true in our spirit. When this happens, we can check the guidance by seeing if it is in line with the principles found in God's Word. If so, consider that this could be the divine guidance you've been seeking.

God can answer our prayers for His wisdom and guidance through unlimited possibilities, so pay attention to the people and opportunities that come your way after you've prayed. Your answer may be right around the corner. When you are not sure about whether you're making a healthy choice, pray repeatedly the *Serenity Prayer* (found earlier in this chapter).

Questions to Answer:

- What do you do when you need to make an important decision?

- Describe a situation where you delayed taking action because you were "waiting" for God's will. What happened?

- Cite an example in which God answered your prayers through another individual or a new experience.

- How important is it for you to have regular daily quiet time for prayer and meditation?

- How does time spent in prayer and meditation affect you?

- What do you need to do to stay aligned with God?

Scriptures Related to Chapter Eleven:

Colossians 3:16	Psalms 25:4-5	Psalms 1:1-3
Mark 11:24	Matthew 7:7	Matthew 21:22
Matthew 6:33		

Prayer for Chapter Eleven:

Dear God,

Help me practice prayer and meditation to become closer to You, that I would better know Your will for my life. Help me seek Your direction in my thinking and actions, and give me freedom from self-seeking motives, dishonesty, fear, and self-pity so that I may help others and carry out what You would give me to do throughout the day. Help me to live in Your peace and love. Amen.

Spreading the Peace . . .

When people are serving,
life is no longer meaningless.
—*John Gardner*

The true meaning of life is to plant trees,
under whose shade you do not expect to sit.
–*Nelson Henderson*

Step 12 helps us live in the solution by helping others and passing on what we have been given.

TWELVE

Passing it On

Pass It On: Keep doing steps 1-11, and tell others readily what God has done for you in your life. *(Galatians 6:1)*

Understanding that God wants us to be of maximum service to others gives us a special sense of purpose and meaning. This is why we've been cleaning up our lives in this process of recovery, and it is in the work of Chapter Twelve that the real spiritual awakening comes, for now we reap the benefits of all the work we've done in the previous chapters. As we heal from insecurities and low self-esteem, as we let go of fear and self-centeredness, as we practice increased conscious connection with God through daily prayer and meditation, we become able to receive God's mystical, unconditional love, and our destiny unfolds.

Chapters One through Eleven gave us the tools by which to grow spiritually. We learned to read and pray in the morning to set the tone of our day; to speak God's truth into our lives; to meditate on His Word; to keep our side of the street clean; and to forgive others. But all of these are only a part of our walk with God. It's our love and faith in Him that pleases Him most. When we walk in faith, we are no longer confused. We trust God; we surrender to Him; and we lean on Him. We don't have to figure things out on our own anymore, and we can look forward to a bright future. That's what keeps us spiritually fit!

Depression, which had plagued me since childhood, followed me into early recovery, despite applying these steps to my life. One year around the Christmas holidays, I was having trouble shaking the depression off. I continued to pray, talk about it, give it to God, and live life the best I could, one day at a time. I clung to the expression, "This too shall pass."

Then one day I went to Wal-Mart. Christmas songs were playing as I walked through aisles stocked with seasonal items and caught sight of a Santa suit for sale. My spirit leaped inside me as I felt the strong urge to buy it.

I immediately questioned myself: *What are you going to do with a Santa suit?* I couldn't imagine why my spirit would leap at the prospect of buying a Santa suit. But I had learned to be obedient to my inner spirit/intuition/God-guidance, no matter how illogical it seemed, so I bought the suit!

The following night, the week before Christmas, I went to a recovery meeting, where I shared about having bought a Santa suit, saying that if anyone needed it, please let me know. After the meeting, an older woman with a slight handicap approached me. She told me her daughter had gone out on drugs again, had been arrested, and was now sitting in jail. This woman's four-year-old grandson was now suddenly in her full-time custody.

She teared up as she spoke of how badly he missed his home and mother, of his pain in having no idea why he was not at home with her. She asked me if I would consider dressing up as Santa and surprising the child with a present she had already bought for him.

Truthfully, in my depression, that was the last thing I felt like doing. Yet, looking into her tear-streaked face, the words, "Sure I will," came out of my mouth. I told her I'd be at her apartment the following day at 4 p.m.

An hour before I was due at her apartment, I started dressing up in the Santa suit. I stuffed pillows around my stomach, around my rear, and anywhere I needed to enlarge myself to take on the persona of the big jolly ole fellow. Glancing in the mirror on my way out the door, I decided that, from a distance, I looked fairly convincing. I felt quite self-conscious, though, and was not in a Santa kind of mood.

It was early afternoon when I walked to the woman's apartment door and knocked. She greeted me and motioned for me to come in. In her living room, the cutest little boy sat on the couch. His eyes opened wide and a big smile of amazement and awe spread across his face. I let out a few "Ho ho ho's!" and called him by name. That was all the proof he needed that I really was Santa Claus. I gave him his present and said I needed to get going to visit thousands of other little children. The truth was, I didn't want to chance his figuring out I was really a five-foot three-inch, forty-something woman struggling with insecurities and a bout of bad depression. The little boy gave me a hug, and I was on my way.

As I was walking to my car, I heard a child's voice yell out, "There's Santa!" I turned around and saw five children running toward me. My heart raced as I fumbled with my car key and unlocked the door. But the children caught up to me just as I was getting into the car. They were eager to tell me what they wanted for Christmas and I listened and assured them I would put their wishes on my list. Just before I drove off, one of the children said, "Santa, why do you have long nails painted red?" I just said a few more "Ho ho ho's!" and "Merry Christmas!" and drove away.

I did not want to be the one to tell them the truth about Santa. As I drove home, I realized that people in passing cars were either waving or honking at me. With my newly acquired ho-ho-ho attitude, I smiled and honked and waved back at them.

When I got home, I ran into the house. Enjoying the reflection in the mirror of myself-as-Santa, I laughed at what I had just done. Then I noticed a surprising thing: I wasn't depressed. I felt lighthearted, like a Santa who had just brought good cheer to a child in need. I had stumbled right into the principle of Chapter Twelve and the solution to depression. All my praying, talking, thinking, and inventorying, alone, had not been the answer. These practices had prepared me for the ultimate solution to my preoccupation with myself: helping someone else.

The following year I volunteered to be Santa at my workplace and brought gifts of candy to the other departments. Everyone laughed, and it was great fun. I began being Santa in a nursing home, at recovery parties, for benefit functions, and wherever I was needed—or, more accurately, whenever I needed it! Years later, my husband filled the Santa outfit, and I ordered a Mrs. Santa suit, and we became a duo for various functions. We even appeared in a televised government meeting one Christmas season.

The Santa suit gave me the freedom to choose the persona of a cheerful giver. But you don't need a costume to become that to others in your life or to uplift your own spirit. The key is to give what we can, using what we have, so that we can keep what our spiritual lives have brought us: love and peace of mind.

Carrying the Message

When we share our experience, strength, and hope, life takes on new meaning. Loneliness vanishes as we see hope grow in others. Our great joy becomes sharing with others the recovery principles we've discovered in these chapters. Paying forward what was given to us secures our growth. It's easy to slip back into old behaviors if we don't practice recovery and keep it fresh in our minds. Helping others requires time and effort. But when we are struggling and don't feel like giving, that is the most important time to do so. Selflessness offers amazing release from being stuck in self-centered fear.

The prayer of St. Francis of Assisi is a beautiful statement of how to become agents of change by carrying the message of love and recovery to others in need. This prayer helps us focus on becoming loving and caring to others instead of remaining self-centered:

Prayer of St. Francis of Assisi

Lord, make me an instrument of your peace!
Where there is hatred—let me sow love;
Where there is injury—pardon;
Where there is doubt—faith;
Where there is despair—hope;
Where there is darkness—light;
Where there is sadness—joy.
O Divine Master, grant that I may not so much seek
to be consoled as to console;
to be understood as to understand;
to be loved as to love.
For it is in giving that we receive;
it is in pardoning that we are pardoned;
and it is in dying that we are born to eternal life. Amen.

Carrying the message can be as simple as when we come across someone suffering as we once did and we share our story as honestly as we can. We can have a brief conversation with that person and explain what our life was like, what happened to us as a result of experiencing God through the principles in this book, and how our lives were changed.

It can happen anywhere—through volunteer work; in sharing one-on-one or in support groups; in our interaction with friends, coworkers, and family members. If you want to be proactive and available to share your testimony, you can go to shelters, churches, and recovery meetings. You can even create a support group.

We need not waste time trying to convince or argue with someone about recovery. If they are not ready, we might turn them off for a future opportunity. We might only plant a seed at this time. Don't work too hard at it. If the other person wants it, she has to do the work.

But if someone is interested, we can share that we couldn't stop our downward spiral on our own. Telling our experiences and our stories is helpful. We talk about our own past problems, hopeless-ness, and loneliness. We share what we were afraid of and how we tried to remedy it. By telling our stories, we assure the other person that there is hope for them, too. We remind them that the key to healing is to couple belief and understanding with action:

Understanding + Belief + Action = Recovery Results

People who have applied these principles often say, "When I first started, had I been given what I asked for, instead of waiting for what God had in mind for me, I would have badly shortchanged myself." What God gives us through recovery is often greater than anything we could have planned, no matter what our circumstances were when we started.

In Chapter Twelve's work, we further our growth by carrying the message of healing to others. In recovery, our painful pasts become a badge of honor by which we can say, "Look what God has done in my life!" The greater the transformation, the greater the joy in recovery. As we do the steps and heal, our level of love, acceptance, honesty, and peace of mind increases. God gives each person a specific call to min-istry. Our gifts may be one or many. Through our healing from pain and suffering, we have learned that what matters most in life is not winning for ourselves; it is changing course to help others.

Becoming a mentor is another way of sharing the message. As mentors, we share what God is doing in our lives; we become God's representatives on earth. That's part of the surrender deal: We become His ambassadors. If you're waiting to be perfect before reaching out to help another, that's never going to happen. When we let God use us, warts and all, for His purposes, we are being a friend to Him. Ask yourself, "Hasn't He been there for me?" The following are some suggestions of what we can do to mentor someone:

• Meet with the person regularly.

• Keep in touch by phone.

- Share your experience, strength, and hope.

- Be a good listener.

- Encourage the other person and offer constructive feedback.

- Make suggestions, but don't ever tell her what to do.

- Make her feel safe by respecting her confidentiality.

- Focus on Scriptures and Bible stories to help her with her relationship with God and others.

- Give her weekly writing assignments to help her discover the simple spiritual steps to living.

- And when God taps you on the shoulder to confront her about unhealthy thoughts and character defects, be prepared to feel the discomfort of her initial reactions. No one likes to hear the truth about herself or her blind spots, but it's the truth that sets us free when we hear it and learn how to act on it.

- Spend time praying with her and for her.

We don't need to worry about knowing what to say. Trust God, and He'll direct our words. We are simply His mouthpiece. Proverbs 3:5-6 tells us, *"Trust in the LORD with all your heart, and lean not on your own understanding; In all your ways acknowledge Him, and He shall direct your paths."*

We can take the pressure off ourselves. If we weren't here for this person, God would have picked someone else to help her. Make no mistake: We are not healing them; God is. Don't give yourself credit for God's work. If the person we are mentoring does well, it's not to our credit. If she does poorly, it's not our fault.

Even if you're afraid to start mentoring, do it anyway, do it afraid! This is not about us, it's about them. The only way to get over fears is to walk through them. It's a privilege to be used as a friend to someone God wants to help. Being of service is the ultimate cure for self-centeredness. We can experience deep joy in helping others, and depression can't survive in the light of joy.

Having a Spiritual Awakening

If we have practiced all the steps, we will have developed a deeper relationship with God. This connection with Him will enable us to see light instead of darkness and view many painful past experiences from a more mature, spiritual perspective. As we gain a new understanding of ourselves as children of God, we acquire an emotional balance to living.

Our human nature often resists being of service. But our spiritual nature, aligned with the will of God, is to reach out and help others, thereby advancing God's Kingdom here on earth.

As we recover and seek God in our lives, we often ask, "What is my purpose on earth?" Sometimes we wonder, "Is this all there is? What happens to us after death? Is Heaven real?" Finding our spiritual identities and forming a relationship with God leads us to our answers to these deep and vital questions.

God promises us that, if we turn to Him while we are here on earth, our lives with Him in Heaven will be full of joy and our pleasures will be forever. (Psalm 16:11) Don't dismiss Heaven with "out of sight, out of mind" thinking. Matthew 6:19-21 tells us to lay up our treasures in Heaven:

> Do not lay up for yourselves treasures on earth, where moth and rust destroy and where thieves break in and steal; but lay up for yourselves treasures in heaven, where neither moth nor rust destroys and where thieves do not break in and steal. For where your treasure is, there your heart will be also.

God tells us that the love we share in this life will contribute to what we experience in the next life. The good we do doesn't go unnoticed, and while we may not receive blessings from our efforts here and now, we will there, later. The more we believe in and live for Heaven, the more motivated we are to follow God's lead; the more we follow God's lead, the more spiritually awakened we become.

The real spiritual awakening of the *Well Woman* boils down to discovering and practicing true love toward God, ourselves, and others. True love doesn't count the costs, but the opportunities. Real love doesn't consider self; it is sacrificial. It serves, gives, and sacrifices for others. True love doesn't ask, *"What have you done for me lately?"*

It takes a spiritual awakening to practice true love. As imperfect human beings, we are incapable of giving real love. Only God can put that kind of sustaining love in one person's heart for another. It's a gift. When we lay down our self-centeredness and self-seeking, which is what separates us from God, then we are truly open to giving and receiving His love. What changes our nature is not that we love God, but that He loved us and poured His Divine love into us.

Applying These Spiritual Principles to Our Everyday Life

Valentine's Day was approaching when I got a call from a woman who was struggling emotionally. She had a lot of painful memories associated with this holiday. Two years earlier her mother had passed away the day before Valentine's Day; the following year, her husband left her on Valentine's Day. As she talked to me, she cried and said she was tired of being alone and that she was dreading Valentine's Day.

As I heard her sadness, a voice in my spirit said, "Tell her to make new Valentine's Day memories by helping others who are feeling what she feels." Instead of remaining stuck in her sadness over the past, we looked at how she could help others in the present. By the end of the phone call, she decided to become an undercover Valentine's Day Angel for people she knew who were lonely or facing difficult challenges.

Since she managed a large apartment complex, she had plenty of folks to pick from. She decided to anonymously deliver flower arrangements, with notes professing God's love, to each person on her list. She would deliver them in the early morning so she could be unseen.

Her experience was a great example of applying Chapter Twelve's principles and helping others. *What she wanted, she became for others. She passed on what she had learned so that she could keep it!* Luke 6:49 warns us to put into practice what we learn or we will lose it: *"But he who heard and did nothing is like a man who built a house on the earth without a foundation, against which the stream beat vehemently; and immediately it fell. And the ruin of that house was great."*

In Chapter Twelve, we seek to be blessed so that we may bless others. Having awakened spiritually to God's love within us, we seek to let it flow through us to others. As we partner with God, He will place people in our path to help and express His love to. Being a channel through which God's miracles flow to others transcends all human reason and logic; these opportunities only occur when we allow Him to use our hands and feet. The beauty is that, as we practice giving to others, the love and confidence inside us grows naturally!

And if you want a loving person in your life, *Well Women*, know that you must become one! We cannot love without giving, and the more anonymous we manage to be, the more God shines through. Kindness is love in action. God has everyone's Wish List, so listen for His direction and be on call for Him twenty-four hours a day.

Below are some ways in which you can get started helping others, sometimes anonymously, through random acts of kindness. By doing these sorts of things in your everyday life, you develop the habit of listening for God's directions for being used to create miracles for others. Become a spy for God, seeking out people whom you can help for Him.

- Clean out your closets and give away whatever you don't use.

- Call someone having a hard time, and just listen.

- Create a spiritual or a recovery support group.

- Buy groceries for a struggling family and anonymously leave the food on their doorstep.

- Call the local shelter for abused women and find out what they need.

- Offer to babysit for a single working parent.

- Keep track of the needs of people you know and connect those who can help each other.

- Send flowers to someone at work who is unrecognized and underpaid. Attach an anonymous note.

- Contribute to a bake sale or garage sale to raise money for a local charity.

- Pay someone's shortage in the grocery store's check-out lane.

- Spontaneously give something of yours to a person who admires it.

- Read a story to someone who can't read.

- Volunteer at your local rehab center.

- Become a Big Sister to some younger person in need.

- Slip some money into an elderly woman's purse when she's not looking.

- Bring some candy or flowers to a nursing home and brighten up a lonely person's day.

- Refill the parking meter when you vacate your parking space.

- Pay for the next person in line at the drive-thru. Ask the cashier to tell the people in the car to have a nice day.

- Keep gift certificates with you for gas or food and be ready to hand them out to someone in need.

- Have extra copies of your favorite inspirational book on hand and be ready to give one away to someone having a hard time.

- Let someone cut in front of you during rush hour traffic—and smile.

- Offer a ride or assistance to a senior citizen struggling with carrying packages.

- Smile!

Doing random acts of kindness takes time away from feeling sorry for ourselves. It helps us see the contrast between a life lived selfishly and one lived for love. Of course, we will all have down moments. Sadness about being alone will still occasionally fill our hearts. But, from here on, we will set a timer! We are allowed only one hour for a pity-party. We can cry all we want for sixty minutes, but then we must put the tissues away and get busy. God and this world need us to begin to grow the light of real love in our spirits. If you don't know where to get started on your first random acts of kindness, simply ask God to put people in your path that He wants to bless through you.

As *Well Women*, we can be a part of God's power, miracles, healings, signs and wonders. He can use us to produce a hundred-fold fruit for His Kingdom. We must not grow weary. To be blessed, and to grow in the scope of the people we reach for Him, consider praying out loud the *Prayer of Jabez* found in, 1 Chronicles 4:10:

> *And Jabez called on the God of Israel saying, "Oh, that You would bless me indeed, and enlarge my territory, that Your hand would be with me, and that You would keep me from evil, that I may not cause pain!' So God granted him what he requested."*

Questions to Answer:

- Write about a concern you had before you began reading this book, and describe your experience of resolving that problem by applying the steps in these twelve chapters.

- How do you practice the principles of these chapters in all your affairs?

- What is the message of hope you have to carry? What promises are coming true for you today?

- How do you remain spiritually awake and fully alive?

- What have you experienced when sharing this program with others in recovery?

- What footprints are you making for others to follow?

Scriptures Related to Chapter Twelve:

Galatians 6:1	Ephesians 5:1-2	Ecclesiastes 4:9-12
2 Timothy 4:2	1 Peter 4:11	Luke 8:16-18

Prayer for Chapter Twelve:

Dear God,

Show me what I can do today for the person who is still suffering. Thank You for keeping me safe wherever I go while carrying out Your will of helping others. Amen.

Endnote . . .

It is good to have an end to journey towards;
but it is the journey that matters in the end.

— Ursula LeGuin

ENDNOTE

Finding True Love

If you've been applying and practicing the principles of these twelve chapters in all your affairs, and are passing on the healing you've been experiencing, then you have become aware that the true love of your life is God. My prayer is that you are developing an intimate relationship with Him.

God has a unique destiny planned for each of us. Some will be called to remain single in this life, married only to God, spiritually. Others will marry good men with whom they will further explore their marriage with God and His unconditional love for us.

The criteria for a healthy, loving relationship is discovering God's love within you and staying spiritually fit. We are called to seek and live out God's will, above all else. Only by doing so can we have a healthy relationship with another human being. God desires that we be made whole and live lives of joy and love. He gives us our heartfelt desires and delights when we obediently follow His lead and allow the unfolding of His special plans and purposes for us. Leaving the results to God's timing and His ways, filled as they are with mystery and wonder, makes unlimited possibilities and dreams come true!

If you have made your peace with being single, then hopefully, as a result of doing the work of these twelve chapters, you are at peace yourself and enjoying your own company. Maybe you are honestly and sincerely okay with being single the rest of your life. I hope you recognize this amazing transformation for the miracle it is. It means you have let go of the fear of abandonment and are no longer willing to settle for less than what is best for you. How can anything top that?

On the other hand, maybe there is someone God has been preparing you for all along. It can be hard for us to imagine what a good, healthy relationship might be like if we've never been in one. That is why it is important to turn not only your *life* but your *love life* completely over to God, letting *Him* choose whether you are to be with someone else, and, if so, with whom.

Consider writing a letter to God, telling Him the kind of mate you would like to have. Get a picture in your mind of what a good, godly man would mean to you. Remember that God wants us to have the best, not the least, so set a high standard. This part of your walk—imagining a godly man—will call on your faith because it probably won't be based on your experiences in past relationships.

As you write your love letter request to God, detail the kind of husband you wish you could have had and the kind of man who would touch your heart. End your letter by requesting God's will and by choosing your highest potentials in life. In the spaces below, address the characteristics and traits you desire in a mate. After the example below, I've included the love letter I myself wrote as a guide to get you thinking:

Dear God,

Here is a description in several categories of the kind of man I think would make a good husband for me. Ultimately, if Your plans for me include having a mate, I want You to choose him for me. I love being married to You, and I have never been happier!

Spiritually:

Mentally:

Emotionally:

Physically:

Career-Profession:

How He Treats Me:

How We Would Spend Our Time Together:

Thank You, God!
Love,

_____

My letter, written to God about my future husband:

Dear God,

Here is a description of the kind of man I think would make a good husband for me. Ultimately, if You have plans for me not to be alone, I want You to choose him for me. I love being married to You, and I have never been happier!

Spiritually*: First and foremost, this man will know and love You. He works a spiritual program, applies the principles of recovery equivalent to a Christian believer's walk. He is responsible, accountable, honest, and his priorities are right, putting God first. He's loyal, disciplined, joyful, and he understands there is a bigger picture. He helps others, prays, meditates, and walks closely with You and knows You as his source. He is not afraid of unlimited opportunities. He is intuitive and listens to his inner voice. He has dealt with the failures of an ego-driven life and has surrendered, instead, to Your Divine will, and he addresses this daily in his life.*

Mentally: *He has a healthy intellect and enjoys talking about his thoughts, insights, and opinions. He is open to new thoughts, ideas, and opinions. He has strong communication skills, is evolved enough to recognize when his thinking is old or inappropriate, and can let it go. He likes to read and write.*

Emotionally: He has worked on getting in touch with his feelings; he embraces and acknowledges his emotions; he is sentimental and sensitive to others; and he is a lover of life. He is enthusiastic, optimistic, and can cry. He can acknowledge and allow other people to have their feelings, and he is strong, stable, and self-aware.

Physically: He has a nice physic, is in shape, is a non-smoker and a non-drinker who exercises and eats healthily. He has dark or salt-'n-pepper hair, looks great in casual clothes or a suit, likes to dress nicely, and can also enjoy wearing a flannel shirt. He's around my age or a little older. He's strong, not wimpy. He can have a sophisticated, updated look. He's smart and has a confident demeanor. He appreciates nice things and he has a nice home and car.

Career-Profession: In some way, he serves the public. His work will in some way compliment my skills and background so that in our careers, we can work together, with that work being based on spiritual awareness. His work requires good communication skills and/or seeks a mate who can contribute her communication and intuitive skills. He has two sides to his nature: One side is very professional; the other is fun-loving and playful. He is ambitious.

How He Treats Me: He gives me the utmost respect. He is understanding and accepting of who I am. He has patience and he is not controlling. He is trustworthy. He is happy to have me in his life. He appreciates me and the love I express for him. He is affectionate and he respects our individuality. He leaves room for each of us to follow God's direction in our lives, individually and corporately. He welcomes and embraces a growing group of family and friends. He is understanding and supportive when I'm "having a growth spurt."

Our Time Together: He likes to travel with me. He also likes to spend quiet time together reading, sitting in front of a fire, or taking a walk in nature. He is peaceful and comfortable talking out a disagreement. Each of us knows that God has brought us into each other's lives as divine opportunities to express the love we have embraced within ourselves and for God. There is a deep, enduring, *easy, comfy, at-home sense of loving each other. We have a deep spirited bond and we know it.*

Thank you God!

Love,

Catherine

P.S. Good luck on filling this tall order. You're the one who taught me to have such high standards and to imagine the best!

P.S.S. Since I don't know what signs to ask for, please use the details in this letter to help me identify the man you send (if you send one).

Now, put your letter away in a lockbox or special place for safekeeping, imagining, as you do so, that you are placing it into God's hands. In your mind and heart, leave it with God. Try to refrain from rereading it. Instead, stay focused on living your life fully with God.

So how does a godly woman find a godly man? She doesn't. He finds her. A hunting instinct takes over in a godly man to find the right woman, and God will lead him in the hunt for you. Your part is to simply live in purity and fullness, doing what God puts in your heart to do, knowing that when God gets ready to bring you a husband, it will be at the right time. You don't need to scout out a man, or to run one down and tackle him. On the other hand, don't accept a man just because he shows up. Only accept him if you have peace in your heart that God has sent him to you. When the stage is set and the time is right, *there will be no doubt.*

You don't have to act out of desperation. Don't jump for anyone. You are a child of God. Wait. Don't make any quick decisions. Take your time. You don't have to be rushed into a relationship you are not ready for. You don't have to settle. Let God give you the "one of His choosing" because God is the ultimate matchmaker.

Remember the standards that you've learned to set as a godly woman! Know your value and your worth before God, because He is your creator and He's your real husband forever. There is no need to have less than that, because you already have the best.

Don't look for true love the way the world does, the way Hollywood does it in the movies: find the right person; fall in love; fix your hopes and dreams on this other person, and expect him to fulfill you—and then, when that inevitably fails, repeat the same pattern over and over, hoping to get it right.

Do it God's way. You've become the right person: You walk in love; you fix your hopes and dreams on *God* for your fulfillment. When you do find yourself in a relationship, you will seek to please God through it. You no longer have to be stuck in the vicious cycle of feeling such loneliness and emptiness in a relationship that is going nowhere.

You're no longer who you used to be. Expect new outcomes. You live in God's Kingdom now, and things turn out differently when God is involved. You don't know what God has up His sleeve!

About Marriage

Keep in mind that, when we first meet our mate, a neurochemical infatuation will kick in that will diminish with time. At most, that delirious passion will last twelve to eighteen months. Infatuation has a blinding effect on how well we see the challenges that exist in the differences between us. If you think the person you're with isn't likely to offend you or push your buttons, give it some time. Wait and see. Don't rush into marriage during this period of infatuation, when your brain is literally incapable of evaluating and thinking clearly about your beloved.

God designed marriage to make us holy rather than just make us happy. If your goal in life is to become like Jesus, marriage will help you by shining a light on your character defects. Marriage is God's way of developing sacrificial, unconditional love in us.

Marriage is especially hard in the beginning because we are two imperfect people trying to love perfectly and become one. Most of us are surprised when we find marriage is much more difficult than we expect. Here's the dilemma: The function of marriage is to teach us *how to love.* God's calling to us is to be unselfish. Yet virtually everyone marries for selfish reasons: to be loved, which we think is our greatest need. But God's purpose for us is different; He wants us *to seek to love*. Our basic need to be loved has been taken care of by God. God first loved us. Learning that when our partner messes up, we don't need to mess up in return is key to a good marriage. Otherwise, we have two fallen people and both go down. We need to stay God-centered and practice not tripping over each other's problems.

In marriage, we learn to put someone else's needs and good above our own. If we think about how God loves, we see how much room we have for growth. And if we look at Jesus's example, we can see *how* to grow. Instead of trying to change our partner so that he will love us better, we look at how we can love him better. If we're asking our spouse to be more than they can be, we are pursuing a marriage that doesn't exist, and our frustration will deepen. When we go into marriage expecting something we can't get, we will be blinded to what it does offer.

God gives us marriage to become more of what we *can* be. Such a marriage provides a space in which we can experience God's patience as we work out our shortcomings. If we don't face and deal with our defects in the marriage we are in, the same issues will follow us out of that marriage and into our next relationship because our same shortcomings will continue to dwell in us.

When we treat our mate well and practice God's ways, we are keeping God in the center. Ecclesiastes 4:12 **tells us that, though one person, alone, may be overpowered by the enemy, two people together can withstand him—and** " . . . *a threefold cord is not quickly broken.*" When two people are united in pursuit of the best for each other, then those two stand together better than one. And when we put God in the middle of the mix, it strengthens the love and foundation of the relationship so that it can weather even the strongest of storms.

When we find ourselves on the brink of a storm with loved ones, family, friends, and coworkers, we can create and maintain healthy relationships—especially with a significant other—by practicing the suggestions below:

- **Stay committed to the process of healing.** Though men and women can be opposites in nature, the Bible says that *"they will become one flesh."* Finding unity and becoming one with your mate takes time and effort.

- **Agree ahead of time to agree to disagree.** Sometimes we will have differing views, opinions, and expectations. When two people look at a quarter held up between them, one sees tails, and the other sees heads. It is the same quarter viewed from different perspectives. Neither is wrong, just different.

- **Don't run out or attack back defensively.** When your mate says something insensitive or in opposition to your thoughts and beliefs, talking it out can calm things down. Often, attack-back verbal responses are just a misdirected cry for help. If you really want your mate to soothe you, to talk with you, to reach out to you with love and reassurance, then look at how you're approaching him! Are you being accusatory before you've heard what he has to say? Are you putting him on the defensive with your tone and attitude? Are you creating a need for your partner to build walls?

- **Practice BACKTRACKING.** You do this when you forgive each other and provide an opportunity for a *do-over.* Allow your partner to backup and try again when they've made a mistake. Choose to let the other person redo the event, to get it right. Then, don't ruin the redo by reminding them about the mistake, over and over again. God never brings up our mistakes; we need to be as forgiving of others.

- **Bring your unsolved problem to God.** When you and your partner are stuck in opposing views and talking it out isn't working, don't get mad. Instead, agree to go to God in prayer and let God make the changes. Only God can get inside people and change them. So He will either change your heart or your partner's, or

He will bring you both into a compromise. Stay open to His wisdom. God will provide solutions that bless your relationship when you put Him first and center.

- **Spend ten minutes telling each other what you love about one another.** The enemy would love to cause dissension in your relationship and split you up. Mistrusting one another, being critical, undermining, and undervaluing each other are schemes the enemy uses. Such divisiveness will create obstacles and distance between you, your partner, and God. When you feel your partner's opposition, instead of getting mad, sad, or irritated, take the word *I* out of your discussions and seek to discover your partner's needs. Keep it positive and speak kind and good words about your partner. It can dismantle the defensive walls and soften the heart.

- **Follow God's instruction 1 Corinthians 13:4-8 on how to love:**

  Love suffers long and is kind; love does not envy; love does not parade itself, is not puffed up; does not behave rudely, does not seek its own, is not provoked, thinks no evil; does not rejoice in iniquity, but rejoices in the truth; bears all things, believes all things, hopes all things, endures all things. Love never fails.

Whether we marry or stay single, we have an exciting destiny ahead. Nothing about God is empty, lonely, and boring. God is love and life. Keep your eyes focused on Him and He will richly fill your heart and experiences with all that you need and with that which is perfect for you!

Appendices . . .

Common Characteristics of an Abused Woman

When we come out of neglectful and dysfunctional homes, we tend to unconsciously seek out mates, in adulthood, who will recreate the abusive treatment we became accustomed to in childhood. We need to heal from the need to recreate old patterns, some of which are:

I don't want to be who I am.

I run from my pain.

I get love mixed up with sex and being desired by men.

I get paralyzed with fear.

I have difficulty speaking up for myself.

I do not feel safe.

I am addicted to the adrenalin rush of chaos and crisis in my life.

I act like a victim.

I can't stop repeating bad relationship patterns.

I have no self-esteem.

I do self-destructive things.

I am harsh, critical, and condemning of myself.

I feel overly responsible for other peoples' problems.

I feel everything is my fault and I apologize incessantly for things.

I don't know how to set boundaries.

I feel guilty standing up for myself.

I isolate from others to deal with my loneliness.

My morality is confused. (I sleep with the wrong people on impulse or out of lust, then marry him to make it right.)

I do in adulthood what I learned in childhood, even though I swore I would make things different.

I have a dependent personality and fear abandonment, yet I repeatedly involve myself with abusive, insensitive, and unavailable men.

My best attempts at change and healing leave me powerless over my unmanageable life.

I continuously find myself moving in the opposite direction of my dreams.

I am desperate, and do not know God or love in my life.

Common Attributes of a Well Woman

God can teach you about becoming a *Well Woman*. It's not too late, regardless of your age or your past. We all have a Spiritual Father in God, and He has equipped spiritual Mothers, *Well Women*, who have walked the road before you and can show you a better way. This is what I have learned from *Well Woman;* that has enabled me to live the dream I thought was lost so many years ago:

Well Women have boundaries. They say no to inappropriate or unacceptable behavior from men.

Well Women do not feel desperate to have another person fill the emptiness inside—they go to God, Who is the only one who can fill us.

Well Women feel comfortable in their own skin. They know their value is not based on poundage, skin firmness, or breast size, but on being a daughter of the Most High God.

Well Women know their source of everything comes from God, and He chooses through whom and how He will provide for us.

Well Women look to God, not to a man, to provide for and protect them.

Well Women know that they will lose anything they put before God, so they don't put a man in God's seat.

Well Women are true to themselves and express their authenticity even if they are afraid.

Well Women have problems, challenges, tragedies, and hardships, but they come through them because their outcomes are controlled by God.

Well Women experience and trust in God's promise, "I can do all things through Christ who strengthens me." (Philippians 4:13)

Well Women look out for other *Well Women* because they have learned they are kindred spirits in the sisterhood. Therefore, they do not sleep with their friends' husbands and boyfriends. Who better understands a woman than another woman?

Well Women have found the one who will never abandon her: God.

Well Women know that *'Rejection is God's Protection!'*

Well Women know they are a catch and do not desperately cling to a love interest who is walking away from them.

Well Women know spiritual peace and will fight to keep it.

Well Women accept that some things may not work out the way they wanted, but trust that things are the way they are for a reason.

Well Women don't have to know the reason *right now.*

Well Women have a support system of at least three: God and at least two wise women friends who know them intimately.

Well Women know the joys of pampering themselves instead of expecting someone else to read their minds.

Well Women have their needs met through their own efforts, God's blessings, and Divine appointments with others over time.

Well Women can't be robbed by man of her joy, peace, love, and security because she receives all this through her intimate relationship with God. The only way she can lose her well-being, once attained, is by giving it up by choice.

Well Women, when they're ready, choose relationships with good men who treat them with love, kindness, and respect.

Well Women hold their men to a high standard of conduct, behavior, and character.

Well Women have learned that it is better to be alone than to be in an unhealthy relationship because she already has a healthy relationship with herself and her Heavenly Husband, God.

Well Women aim to make decisions based on wisdom, guidance, and faith in God, rather than on fear and desperation.

Well Women think through and weigh the consequences of potential choices. They don't jump impulsively out of fear and people-pleasing. They have learned to be true to themselves and they aim at doing the next right thing through lots of practice and hard lessons.

Well Women know that the qualities they would look for in a man must be developed in themselves, first. So a *Well Woman* focuses on herself instead of looking for a *broken partner in need of fixing in hopes of "future potential."*

Well Women create for themselves and/or their children stability; therefore, they don't accept less than stability in a partner.

Well Women educate themselves about the difference between love and lust. Then they makes choices that line up with love. (See 1 Corinthians 13)

APPENDIX III

12 Spiritual Steps to Becoming
a Well Woman

The following steps, based on Biblical principles, can transform your life and help you make peace with God, yourself, and others, and teach you how to keep the peace. They can help you give up your old ways, clean up your connection to the past, make up with people in your present, and keep up with your highest good and unfolding destiny:

1. Admit It   Confess your need for help; admit that you and your life are unmanageable. Write a brief description of how you got to where you are, beginning with your first relationship with your dad and/or mom. *(Romans 7:18)*

2. Believe It   Acknowledge (recognize) that God is greater than you and that He wants you to live. *(Philippians 2:13)*

3. Decide It   Make a decision to live and surrender your life to God. *(Romans 12:1)*

4. Inventory It   Make an inventory (an account) of the resentments and fears in your relationships over the course of your life, starting in childhood. *(Lamentations 3:40)*

5. Tell It   Tell God, yourself, and someone else all about you and your inventory. *(James 5:16a)*

6. Prepare   Get ready for God to take away your character defects. Decide you want to change and believe that God can and will accomplish this change in you. *(James 4:10)*

7. Ask God	Ask God to help you change. Let God heal you, forgive you and love you. Accept the changes that He makes in you. *(1 John 1:9)*
8. Make a List	Make a list of whomever you have hurt, and put yourself on the top of that list. Briefly describe whom you hurt and what you did. Don't look at what they did to you; just focus on what you did to them. *(Luke 6:31)*
9. Make Amends	Let God lead you to making past wrongs right so that you don't have to hide out from anyone. Fix what you can without hurting anyone in the process. *(Matthew 5:23-24)*
10. Maintain	Accept that you will make mistakes. Make daily spot checks and, when you mess up, fix them as soon as possible. Continue to trust and obey God so that you can maintain the changes He makes in you. *(1 Corinthians 10:12)*
11. Pray and Meditate	Seek contact with God through prayer and meditation. Let Him, who is greater than you, show you how to live and guide you through life. *(Colossians 3:16a)*
12. Pass It On	Keep doing steps 1-11, and tell others readily what God has done for you in your life. *(Galatians 6:1)*

God's Promises for Well Women

God promises us a new life as He heals and renews our mind and emotions through His Spirit and His Word. He offers us hope, peace, honor, protection, and love in exchange for our past sins and misery. While there are thousands of promises in the Bible, here are a few key lifesaving promises God gives us and stands by:

Promise of Protection

Isaiah 54:17: *"No weapon formed against you shall prosper . . ."*

Promise of Hope

Jeremiah 29:11: *"For I know the plans I have for you,"* declares the LORD, *"plans to prosper you and not to harm you, plans to give you hope and a future."* (NIV)

Promise of Healing

Isaiah 53:5: *". . . And by His stripes we are healed."*

Promise of Provision

Matthew 6:33: *"But seek first the kingdom of God and His righteousness, and all these things shall be added to you."*

Promise of Fulfillment

Psalm 37:4: *"Delight yourself also in the LORD, And He shall give you the desires of your heart."*

Promise of Peace

John 14:27: *"Peace I leave with you, My peace I give to you; not as the world gives do I give to you. Let not your heart be troubled, neither let it be afraid."*

Promise of Recompense for Your Shame

Isaiah 61:7: *"Instead of your shame you will receive a double portion, and instead of disgrace you will rejoice in your inheritance. And so you will inherit a double portion in your land, and everlasting joy will be yours."*

Promise of Honor

1 Samuel 2:30: *". . . But now the LORD says: 'Far be it from Me; for those who honor Me I will honor, and those who despise Me shall be lightly esteemed."*

Promise of Love

2 Chronicles 16:9: *"For the eyes of the LORD run to and fro throughout the whole earth, to show Himself strong on behalf of those whose heart is loyal to Him."*

Promise of Forgiveness

2 Chronicles 7:14: *". . . if My people who are called by My name will humble themselves, and pray and seek My face, and turn from their wicked ways, then I will hear from heaven, and will forgive their sin and heal their land."*

Promise of Rest

Matthew 11:28-29: *"Come to Me, all you who labor and are heavy laden, and I will give you rest. Take My yoke upon you and learn from Me, for I am gentle and lowly in heart, and you will find rest for your souls."*

Promise of Restoration

Romans 8:28 : *"And we know that all things work together for good to those who love God, to those who are the called according to His purpose."*

Promise of Salvation

Psalm 103:12: *"As far as the east is from the west, so far has He removed our transgressions from us."*

Promise of Prosperity

1 Corinthians 2:9: "But as it is written: *'Eye has not seen, nor ear heard, nor have entered into the heart of man the things which God has prepared for those who love Him.'"*

Promise of Freedom

John 8:32: *"And you shall know the truth, and the truth shall make you free."*

Promise of Sound Mind / Stability

2 Timothy 1:7: *"For God has not given us a spirit of fear, but of power and of love and of a sound mind."*

Promise of No Abandonment

Joshua 1:5: *"No man shall be able to stand before you all the days of your life; as I was with Moses, so I will be with you. I will not leave you nor forsake you."*

Promise of Joy

Psalm 19:11: *"You will show me the path of life; In Your presence is fullness of joy; At Your right hand are pleasures forevermore."*

Promise of Miracles

Matthew 19:26: *"But Jesus looked at them and said to them, 'With men this is impossible, but with God all things are possible.'"*

Slogans for Well Women

The following are some of my favorite and helpful slogans. These slogans are powerful thoughts condensed into simple phrases that can remind you of some deep spiritual truths to turn around your thinking back into God's ways and direction.

Let Go and Let God

You are not alone.

One day at a time.

Live and let live.

First things first.

Look for the good.

By the grace of God.

Know yourself—be honest.

This too shall pass.

Keep it simple.

I can't, He can, I think I'll let Him.

It works if you work it!

We are only as sick as our secrets.

To keep it you have to give it away!

I have a choice.

Don't quit 5 minutes before the miracle happens.

Well Woman Support/Discussion Group Guideline Suggestions

Getting involved with others in recovery for the purpose of support and sharing will accelerate your growth, love, and healing. If you are interested in forming your own *Well Woman* support group, I have put together some guidelines I've found helpful based on my own experience and from attending many successful support groups in recovery:

Finding a Place:

You can choose to have your group meet in a home, a local center, a church, a library or in a hotel meeting room. You'll need chairs and a table, a basket for donations, and paper and pens so that you can write down names and phone numbers for a phone list. You can offer coffee, water, or refreshments.

Getting The Word Out:

The cheapest way to start is through word of mouth. Tell your friends to tell their friends, co-workers, and family. Many local newspapers will list your meeting free of charge as a public service, as long as there is no charge to attend the meeting. The same may be true of your local cable T.V. station. You could create flyers stating information about your gathering. Make sure you give the time, place, purpose of the gathering, and a phone number people can call for directions and information. Distribute the flyers to local bookstores, health food stores, shelters, and other recovery meeting places. You can take out a small ad in the local paper. An example might be:

Well Women's Spiritual Support Group Meeting for the purpose of making new friends, sharing, and growth. Tuesday evenings @ 7:30—8:30 p.m. For more information call...

Suggested Meeting Format:

Have a group facilitator for each meeting. Encourage members to take turns as the facilitator so that no one person tries to dominate the group. A facilitator is someone who gently guides the group to stay on track with its format, making sure people don't interrupt each other, and who keeps track of the time. One-hour meetings are suggested and it is helpful to hold the group to that. If anyone needs more time, encourage her to meet with others after the meeting. Most people feel a little nervous and alone when they first arrive. Designate yourself or others to greet newcomers. Help them feel comfortable and welcome.

A suggested format I've used in my groups:

"Hello. My name is (*your first name*). Welcome to (*name of meeting*).

"Please be sure all cell phones are turned off during the meeting.

"We meet to share our experience, strength, and hope and to offer love and support to one another in our different stages of growth and healing. We do this by seeking God, applying His principles of recovery, and helping each other. We find freedom from the effects of our past and the abuse we lived with, and we learn to have a new life with healthy relationships with God, ourselves, and others, one day at a time.

"Would you please join me in a moment of silence, followed by the Serenity Prayer.

The Serenity Prayer
God grant me the serenity to accept the things I cannot change,
courage to change the things I can, and
wisdom to know the difference. Amen.

"I've asked _____ to read **Common Characteristics of an Abused Woman**.

"I've asked _____ to read **Common Attributes of a Well Woman**.

"I've asked _____ to read **12 Spiritual Steps to Becoming a Well Woman**.

"If you are attending this meeting for the first time, will you please introduce yourself by your first name, so we may welcome you? (Pause.) We are glad you are here. May we go around the room and introduce ourselves by our first name?

My name is _____ .

"Many of us stuck in the cycle of bad relationships and abuse have difficulty recognizing why we stay in them and how to get free of them. Most of the dysfunction in our lives today stems from what we learned in our childhood. We may appear to be adults, but there is a wounded, fearful, hurting child still living in our adult interactions. Together, as we seek God and His love, and apply His ways to our everyday lives, a healing of our inner child occurs and our true adult self begins to emerge.

"We encourage you to limit your sharing to about five minutes so that everyone who wants to share gets a chance to do so. Our meetings are to be a safe place to share your adult and childhood experiences without being judged, and we encourage you to share openly about your experiences.

"Confidentiality is a main ingredient to creating a safe place for sharing with one another. We ask that nothing you hear at this meeting be repeated outside this room.

"We do not allow crosstalk during the meeting. Crosstalk refers to interrupting others while they're talking, or making comments, critiques, or judgments about what another person shares. It also means speaking to an individual directly, instead of to the group as a whole. We do not tell each other what to do, but we base our sharing on our own experience, strength, and hope. This helps us practice taking more responsibility for our own lives, while offering acceptance of where someone else is on her path.

"Today's meeting is about _____ (*Announce your chosen topic for discussion, or ask if someone needs to have a particular subject discussed; or choose a reading out of **Becoming a Well Woman, Way of the Well Woman, God Calling Devotional,** or the **Bible**.)*

"We will begin sharing now and will end at _____ (*approximately five minutes before the close of the meeting*)."

(**The** *Facilitator can call on people who raise their hands, or you can go around the room—**leader's or meeting's choice**.*)

Group sharing ends.

(*Pass the basket for donations five minutes before close of meeting.*) "We will now pass the basket for donations, which will be used to cover any cost of refreshments, rent, or the purchase of books or resource material.

"Does anyone have any recovery related announcements for the group?

"Thank you for being here, and please come back. If you did not have a chance to share, please speak to someone after the meeting if you need to talk.

"It is time to read **God's Promises for Well Women**.

"Will everyone please hold hands and join in closing the meeting with the Lord's Prayer (Matthew 6:9-13):

Our father, who art in Heaven,
Hallowed be thy name.
Your Kingdom come, Your will be done,
On earth as it is in Heaven.
Give us this day our daily bread,
And forgive us our debts,
As we forgive our debtors.
And lead us not into temptation,
But deliver us from evil,
For thine is the kingdom,
the power and the glory forever. Amen.

RECOMMENDED READING

There are many wonderful, informative books on healing from abuse to creating healthy relationships. The books I have listed, are the basic spiritual mainstays of my daily bread that I highly recommend to be used as references to building a strong spiritual foundation, from which you can add your own favorites to. God's ageless wisdom and guidance are found in:

Easy to Read Translations of the Bible are:
The Life Recovery Bible (New Living Translation) Tyndale House Publishers, Inc. 1998 Wheaton, Illinois 60189

The Holy Bible New International Version (NIV) By International Bible Society Published by Zondervan, 1984 Grand Rapids, Michigan 49530 www.zondervan.com

The Amplified Bible Published by Zondervan, 1987 Grand Rapids, Michigan 49530 www.zondervan.com

A God Inspired Book Describing the Solution to Addiction through a Spiritual Program of Living:
The Big Book Alcoholics Anonymous World Services, Inc. 2001 AA General Services Office 212 870-3400 www.aa.org

An Informative and Spiritually Inspired Book About Healing From Growing Up With Neglect, Dysfunction, and/or Alcoholism:
Adult Children of Alcoholics Adult Children of Alcoholics World Service Organization, 2006 Post Office Box 3216 Torrance, CA 90510 www.adultchildren.org

A God Breathed Daily Devotional:
God Calling Authored by The Two Listeners Barbour Publishing, Inc., 1989 P.O. Box 719, Uhrichsville, Ohio 44683 www.barbourbooks.com

SAFETY EXIT PLAN FROM DOMESTIC VIOLENCE

Planning a safe exit from an abusive relationship is important before breaking the ties with your partner. The National Domestic Violence Hotline suggests following these steps to improve your chances of leaving safely.

Checklist

What you need to take when you leave:

Identification:
☐ Driver's License
☐ Birth Certificate
☐ Children's Birth Certificates
☐ Social Security Cards

Financial
☐ Money and/or credit cards (in your name)
☐ Checking and/or savings account books

Legal Papers
☐ Protective Order
☐ Lease, rental agreement and house deed
☐ Car registration and insurance papers
☐ Health and life insurance papers
☐ Medical records for you and your children
☐ School records
☐ Work permits/Green Card/Visa
☐ Passport
☐ Divorce and custody papers
☐ Marriage license

Other

☐ Medications
☐ House and car keys
☐ Valuable jewelry
☐ Address book
☐ Pictures and sentimental items
☐ Change of clothes for you and your children
☐ Other

Emergency numbers

Police Emergency Number 911

National Domestic Violence Hotline
1-800-799-SAFE (7233)
1-800-787-3224 (TTY) for the Deaf

Women's Advocacy Project
Family Violence Hotline
1-800-374-HOPE (4673)

Department of Family and
Protective Services
Abuse/Neglect Hotline
1-800-252-5400

Telephone numbers in your area

Police and/or Sheriff's Department _____

County and/or District Attorney's _____

Office _____

Family Violence Program Hotline _____

Hospital _____

Safety in your own residence:

A. If you stay in your home, lock your windows and change the locks on your doors as soon as possible.

B. Develop a safety plan with your children for times when you are not with them.

C. Inform your children's school, day care, etc., about who has permission to pick up your children.

D. Inform neighbors and the landlord that your partner no longer lives with you, and that they should call the police if they see him/her near your home.

E. Never tell the abuser where you live. Never call the abuser from your home because the abuser may find out where you live.

F. Request an unlisted/unpublished number from the telephone company.

Safety on the job and in public:

A. Inform someone at work of your situation. Include the security officers at work and provide them with a picture of your batterer.

B. Have someone screen your telephone calls at work.

C. Have someone escort you to and from your car, bus or train.

D. Use a variety of routes to come and go from home.

Safety during an explosive incident:

A. If there is an argument; try to be in a place that has an exit and not in a bathroom, kitchen or room that may contain weapons.

B. Practice getting out of your home safely. Identify which doors, windows, elevator, or stairwell to use.

C. Pack a bag, and have it ready at a friend's or relative's house.

D. Identify one or more neighbors you can tell about the violence, and ask them to call the police if they hear a disturbance coming from your home.

E. Devise a code word to use with your children, family, friends and neighbors when you need the police.

F. Decide and plan where you will go if you ever have to leave home.

G. Use your instincts and judgment. In some dangerous situations, give the abuser what he wants to calm him down.

Remember, you don't deserve to be hit or threatened! Safety when preparing to leave:

A. Open a checking or savings account in your own name.

B. Leave money, an extra set of keys, copies of important documents and extra clothes and medicines in a safe place or with someone you trust.

C. Get your own post office box.

D. Identify a safe place where you can go and someone who can lend you money.

E. Always keep the shelter phone number, a calling card, or some change for emergency phone calls with you.

F. If you have pets, make arrangements for them to be cared for in a safe place.

Remember, leaving your batterer is the most dangerous time! Safety with a protective order:

A. If you or your children have been threatened or assaulted, you can request a protective order from the District/County Attorney's Office.

B. Always keep your protective order with you.

C. Call the police if your partner violates the protective order.

D. Inform family members, friends and neighbors that you have a protective order in effect.

E. Think of alternative ways to keep safe if the police do not respond immediately.

You have a right to be safe!

No one deserves to be hit or threatened. If you are being hurt by someone you love, make plans and take precautions to keep yourself and your children safe. Here are some suggestions that have helped other people in situations like yours.

For more information, please visit the Website for the National Domestic Violence Hotline at www.thehotline.org. If you or someone you know is frightened about something in your relationship, please call the National Domestic Violence Hotline at 1-800-799-SAFE (7233).

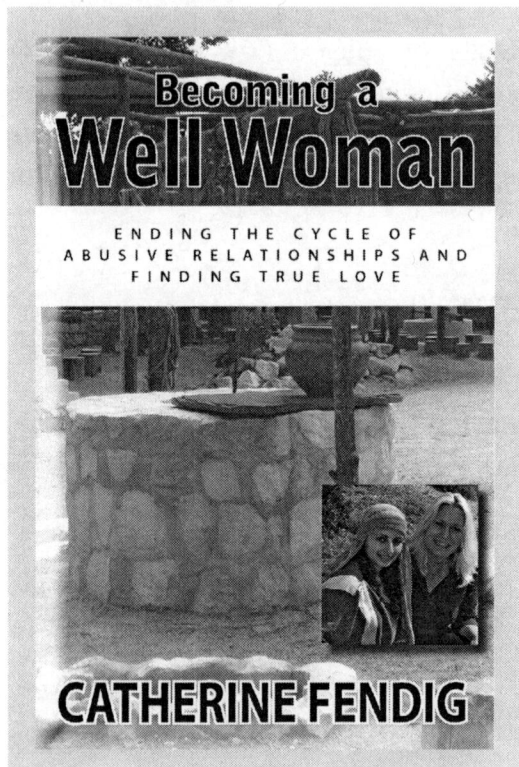

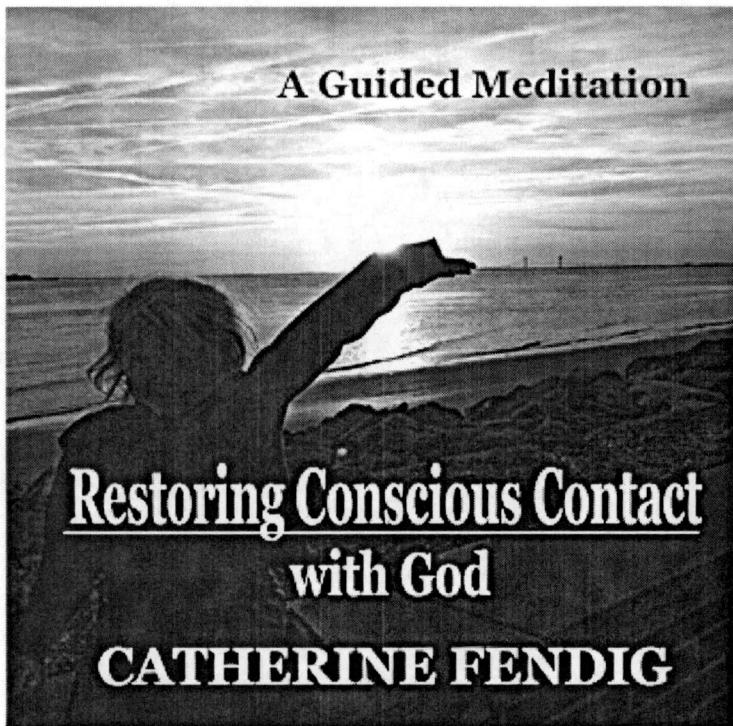

CPSIA information can be obtained at www.ICGtesting.com
Printed in the USA
LVOW100322180413

329753LV00002B/65/P